The Balancing Act

The Balancing Act

Quota Hiring in Higher Education

George C. Roche III

Open Court   La Salle   Illinois

Library of Congress Cataloging in Publication Data

Roche, George Charles.
 The balancing act.

  1. Faculty integration—United States. 2. Higher education and state—United States. I. Title
   LB233w.6.R62   658.31'1   74-11130
   ISBN 0-87548-305-4

To Muriel and Maggie. May they and all the members of their generation have the opportunity to be judged on the basis of their individual merit.

Contents

Foreword

I N RECENT decades, American colleges and universities have inflicted upon themselves a variety of follies. But the most baneful foolishness from which college presidents and professors suffer just now is called "Affirmative Action." It is thrust upon the campus by the federal Office of Civil Rights, and it is ferociously anti-intellectual. Even the Academy of Lagado would have risen up indignantly at such an insult to the higher learning.

To put the matter succinctly, "Affirmative Action" is a program for compelling colleges to engage unqualified or underqualified persons as professors of arts and sciences, merely because those favored persons are alleged to belong to "minorities"—such as women, who form a "minority" amounting to some 51 percent of the American population. Behind this inanity is the force of law. It is an extreme form of the degradation of the democratic dogma.

But I leave analysis of this scheme to Dr. George Roche, the young president of Hillsdale College, a history scholar of some influence. President Roche has been one of the more courageous and intelligent champions of true academic freedom: that is, freedom of college and university from the dictation of political powers or of other forces which possess no rightful authority over the works of the mind. Because his own college accepts no governmental subsidies or grants, Dr. Roche can write with some degree of impartiality: for the present, at least,

Hillsdale College cannot be intimidated by the Department of Health, Education, and Welfare. (Such institutions as Columbia University and the University of Michigan enjoy no such immunity, for they have taken HEW's shilling.)

Dr. Roche is firmly opposed to academic discrimination against present or potential professors on the grounds of sex or of ethnic and racial origins; and his college has an unusually large proportion of women, for instance, in professional and administrative posts. But he is just as strongly opposed to arbitrary political interference with college faculties, and to a "reverse discrimination" which penalizes the competent and rewards the incompetent in the Academy. He is accurate, temperate, and witty.

According to the half-concealed logic of the Affirmative Action program, not more than 3 percent of the professors and instructors (or maintenance men) on any campus should be Jews; or, to carry this reasoning a little farther, about 88 percent of the faculty at Howard University, say, should be white, or at least non-black. The principles of the Office of Civil Rights, consistently applied, would strike out intellectuality as a requirement for the higher teaching, and would substitute sex and color and ancestry as the requisite qualities. This policy obviously violates federal civil rights statutes; but Mr. Stanley Pottinger and his colleagues at HEW, themselves flagrant violators, are in charge of enforcement of those statutes.

A mad world, my masters. Dr. Roche aspires to dispense some sanity among us.

RUSSELL KIRK

Acknowledgment

AFFIRMATIVE ACTION is a federal program intended to suppress discrimination in higher education. What it achieves in actuality is the opposite. It is in fact forcing colleges and universities to practice racial and sexual discrimination in hiring, admissions, and other areas. Many distinguished professors and commentators have spoken out against the mushrooming threat Affirmative Action poses to the academic community and to higher education. Their contributions have been immensely helpful in the preparation of this study. Individual recognition of those whose efforts made this book possible would necessitate a list of unreasonable length. Instead, let me simply offer my thanks to all those whose insights and critical analyses fill these pages.

In the preparation of the manuscript, I owe special thanks to Clark Durant and Llewellyn Rockwell, who played a substantial role in assembling the materials which have become available on Affirmative Action. I am also indebted to Mr. Rockwell and to Dr. Louis Pitchford for their perceptive editorial advice on the manuscript.

Finally, a word of appreciation is due my secretaries, Mrs. Patricia DuBois and Miss Carolyn Spencer, without whose patient, generous and highly competent assistance neither this project nor any of my other undertakings would ever see the light of day.

GEORGE ROCHE
HILLSDALE COLLEGE, MICHIGAN

AUGUST 1974

What is Affirmative Action?

We have a whale of a lot of power, and we're prepared to use it
if necessary.

J. Stanley Pottinger

I N DECEMBER 1972 Columbia University announced,
"We would like to have been able to make copies
of the full-text edition of Columbia University's Affirmative Action Program available to interested parties
without cost. However, because of the expense involved
in reproducing, collating, binding, packing, and handling
this 316 page, 3-1/2 pound document, we are making it
available at $17.25 per copy, which includes postage."

If an interested party were to send for a copy of this
document, though it is difficult to imagine who might be

interested, he would receive a bureaucratized and computerized flood of trivia about the inner workings of Columbia University—more than most observers could conceivably want. The vast outpouring of time and energy necessary to gather and evaluate this information on institutional policy symbolizes a major crisis for Columbia, a crisis given public airing by its administrators.

Columbia University is not alone in its anguish. Other institutions of higher learning across the nation are suffering similar problems as they rush headlong to comply with the Department of Health, Education, and Welfare guidelines imposing racial and sexual quotas on campus. They find they are obliged to hire directors of Affirmative Action Planning at substantial salaries, and set up Affirmative Action programs with policy influence over every aspect of campus life. Such schools as Cornell, Duke, Vanderbilt, Dartmouth, Johns Hopkins, the state universities of Illinois, Michigan, Missouri, and North Carolina are among the growing number of public and private institutions already on the road toward Affirmative Action compliance.

Federal Funding as a Weapon

In a typical Affirmative Action project, the Department of Health, Education, and Welfare (HEW) has demanded that the City University of New York (the largest urban educational institution in the nation, with over 221,000 students and 16,000 staff members) comply with all HEW guidelines, set up an appropriate master plan, and provide complete information to the Office of Civil Rights (OCR), including access to all personnel files by OCR representatives. If this seems a substantial demand, substantial powers of enforcement lie behind the demand. HEW has warned the City University of New York (CUNY) that, should there be failure to comply, "sanctions may include the termination, suspension, or cancellation of existing contracts and subcontracts held by the university and debarment of the university from future receipt of contracts and subcontracts." In short, CUNY has been told by the Office of Civil Rights that complete employment information and evidence of institutional restructuring along HEW-approved racial and sexual lines must be forthcoming, lest HEW sanctions (involving loss of some $13 million in federal research contracts) be invoked.

For over a year before being put on public notice, CUNY had been attempting to move toward racial and sexual hiring quotas—not rapidly enough, however, for the man who was then chief administrator of OCR, Mr. J. Stanley Pottinger. Mr. Pottinger announced at a news conference that CUNY was being put "on clear notice" that "continued non-cooperation" would lead to sanctions.

Affirmative Action, under the auspices of HEW and OCR, has blossomed into a bureaucratic nightmare. Backed by the full force of Labor Department Revised Order #4, HEW and OCR have, since 1971, developed enforcement procedures which reflect a political attempt to mold the hiring practices for America's colleges and universities. American higher education is particularly vulnerable to this assault, since the federal government now disperses contract funds among colleges and universities which run to billions of dollars a year. The funding continues to grow. The Carnegie Commission on Higher Education has recently urged that federal funding to higher education be increased still further within the next six years to some $13 billion a year.

Some of America's most prestigious institutions are already deeply committed to the continued receipt of federal funding. The University of California budget calls for federal contract funds in the vicinity of $72 million a year, the University of Michigan is involved in federal funding to the tune of $60 million, and similar dependence is evidenced by other first-line schools on a level comparable with Princeton, Columbia, and Harvard.

According to HEW figures, federal funding necessitates compliance with OCR guidelines on 2,500 of the nation's 3,000 campuses. The majority of those campuses approached to date have been rushing to comply. This rush to racist and sexist quotas in higher education is being implemented on most campuses by men and women who think of themselves as liberal, who customarily (not to say ritually) voice their commitment to the open society in which individuals would presumably be judged exclusively on the basis of their merits. At least one of the reasons for the dramatic reversal which has occurred must surely be the increasing dependence on federal funding in recent years.

One of the first schools to feel HEW pressures for Affirmative Action was Columbia University, where roughly one-half of the $175 million annual budget is federal money. The 1971 HEW assault astonished Columbia officials who felt that they ". . . had been making very serious efforts during recent years to keep the university abreast of rapidly moving patterns of social change in New York City. . . ." As Columbia President William McGill put it, "In all respects Columbia's record in the field of Affirmative Action to remove employment discrimination seemed to me to be an outstanding one. Nevertheless the government chose to move against us. . . . No one likes to be in the position of negotiating for his survival with Uncle Sam sitting at the other end of the table. Our instincts in such circumstances were to promise almost anything in order to get the government off Columbia's back.''

The special irony of the present situation is that only a few years ago the very academics who today are under such enormous pressure from HEW were the same people who scoffed at the idea that federal money might bring federal control to higher education.

The New Discrimination

Nevertheless, control has come, and with it flagrant discrimination on a nationwide scale. HEW itself has been careful to avoid setting quotas, since such quotas would be in clear violation of the Civil Rights Act. Instead, colleges and universities have been setting their own quotas in a feverish rush to comply with federal pressures. As the result, some strange policies, new to the American academic scene, are now very much in evidence. Vast amounts of time and money are being poured into Affirmative Action programs. Complicated surveys examining the ethnic backgrounds of faculty members are being undertaken. Announcements of job openings appearing in professional circles openly mention specific racial, sexual, or ethnic ''qualifications'' for employment. *De facto* discrimination is now commonplace:

"The Department of Philosophy at the University of Washington is seeking qualified women and minority candidates for faculty positions at all levels beginning Fall Quarter 1973. . . ."

"We desire to appoint a Black or Chicano, preferably female. . . ."

"Dear Sir: The Department of Economics at Chico State is now just entering the job market actively to recruit economists for the next academic year. . .Chico State College is also an affirmative action institution with respect to both American minority groups and women. Our doctoral requirements for faculty will be waived for candidates who qualify under the affirmative action criteria."

"Dear Colleague: Claremont Men's College has a vacancy in its. . .Department as a result of retirement. We desire to appoint a black or Chicano, preferably female. . . ."

"I should very much appreciate it if you could indicate which of your 1972 candidates are either Negro or Mexican American."

"Dear. . .: We are looking for females. . .and members of minority groups. As you know, Northwestern along with a lot of other universities is under some pressure. . .to hire women, Chicanos, etc."

"Your prompt response to my letter of May 12 with four candidates, all of whom seem qualified for our vacancy, is greatly appreciated. Since there is no indication that any of them belong to one of the minority groups listed, I will be unable to contact them. . . ."

"Dear Mr. . . .: All unfilled positions in the university must be filled by females or blacks. Since I have no information regarding your racial identification, it will be possible for me to contact you for a position only in the event you are black."

Only a few years ago, such hiring practices would have been denounced as racist and discriminatory, yet today they find wide acceptance throughout the academic community. How did this change occur?

Legal History

The Office of Civil Rights derives its claim to authority, via HEW, from the Department of Labor, which in turn bases its authority on Executive Order 11246 which was signed by Lyndon Johnson in 1965 pursuant to the Civil Rights Act of 1964. There are good reasons for doubting that President Johnson or anyone else connected with the original civil rights legislation and its implementation anticipated the extent to which middle-echelon bureaucrats would pervert antidiscrimination legislation into discriminatory programs. Yet this is exactly what has occurred.

Originally "affirmative action" was little more than a political slogan, first used by President Kennedy to urge correction of various civil and economic handicaps experienced by minorities in federal employment. By the Johnson years, the slogan was beginning to appear with greater frequency during debate on the Civil Rights Act. During Senate hearings on the act, the fear was expressed that the powers being considered might be later used to force discriminatory hiring. At the time, the fears were dismissed and the act passed.

Though the final draft of the 1964 Civil Rights Act did not mention the phrase, "affirmative action" continued to find its way into discussions of enforcement tactics for the legislation. It was suggested that overall racial proportions should be used as evidence measuring intent and performance of institutions covered by the Civil Rights Act. Presumably such "evidence" would allow the enforcing federal officials to bypass the slow process of individual court cases and thus deal directly with discriminatory situations. In the mid 1960s, even the most outspoken proponents of the concept saw racial proportions as only one indicator of possible discrimination. "Equal opportunity" was still the ultimate goal and quotas were only a specific means to that general end.

As the 1960s wore on, that distinction between means and ends became increasingly obscure. When President Johnson issued his 1967 executive order calling for affirmative action to eliminate employment discrimination among federal contractors, the stage was set for increasing implementation of the quota system. Revised Order #4 was issued by the Department of Labor only months after the Johnson executive order, presumably as an "implementation" of the executive order. But Revised Order #4 did far more. It converted the executive order's original non-discriminatory intent into a weapon to enforce discriminatory hiring:

> An acceptable affirmative action program must include an analysis of areas within which the contractor is deficient in the utilization of minority groups and women, and further, goals and timetables to which the contractor's good faith efforts must be directed to correct the deficiencies and thus, to increase materially the utilization of minorities and women, at all levels and in all segments of his work force where deficiencies exist.

Affirmative Action now began enforcement of the same preferential discrimination on the basis of race and sex which had been expressly forbidden by the Civil Rights Act. Percentage hiring goals, first imposed upon the construction industry in the "Philadelphia Plan" and the "Long Island Plan," spread quickly to racial and sexual quotas for other industrial hiring and then moved throughout the American business community. Meanwhile, enforcement of Revised Order #4 in federal dealings with colleges and universities was delegated by the Labor Department to HEW. By late 1971, Affirmative Action had arrived on the campus.

The Office of Civil Rights has handled HEW enforcement of the program for colleges and universities. Complete records for all employment practices are required of those institutions under examination. This in itself has caused consternation in many schools where confidential employment records have customarily been safe from external scrutiny. Another difficulty has arisen from the fact that most academic employment forms do not require racial information, both because laws in many states specifically forbid the practice and because most colleges and universities have in recent years shown little interest in questions of race or national origin when recruiting their professors. As the result, the Office of Civil Rights, exerting pressure for employment statistics which do not exist, has forced a number of schools into such bizarre antics as judging racial or ethnic origin by analyzing the name or physical appearance of a professor. For this reason, there has been great emphasis upon "candidates with Spanish or Indian surnames," "visual surveys" of faculty, and similarly penetrating means of analyzing a collegiate teaching staff.

However bizarre the means, the Office of Civil Rights has the power to push on toward its end. A college or university may have its Affirmative Action analysis and programs rejected again and again, with the threat of contract cancellation always available as a club to insure compliance.

Resistance to Quotas

There have been some notable efforts within the academic community to resist OCR pressures. However, many institutions seem to protest less as a matter of principle than as the result of a feared inability to comply with HEW demands and thus risk loss of federal funding. The general feeling seems to be that the OCR demands are more objectionable in tone than intent. The bureaucratic arrogance which accompanies Affirmative Action programs is apparently a new experience for many American educators and they have been almost uniformly unenthusiastic.

A protest with greater meaning has come from a relatively small group of educational leaders who are resisting the quota system on principle. Professor Sidney Hook's Committee on Academic Nondiscrimination and Integrity has attracted the support of some 500 scholars, including such major figures as Bruno Bettelheim of Chicago, Nathan Glazer of Harvard, and Eugene Rostow of Yale, all convinced that Affirmative Action as presently proposed will be extremely harmful to academic standards throughout higher education. Through the strong stand taken by these professors and by other groups such as the University Center for Rational Alternatives under the direction of Miro Todorovich, some reversals of Affirmative Action discrimination have been achieved.

The case of W. Cooper Pittman, a doctoral candidate at George Washington University who was caught in the web of Affirmative Action, shows what can be achieved by a principled stand. Pittman's story begins with a letter he received August 16, 1972, stating:

The recommendation for your appointment to the department of psychology at Prince George's Community College was disapproved by the board of trustees on August 15, 1972. The basis for disapproval was primarily that the position presently vacant in that department requires certain qualifications regarding the overall profile of the institution and department as well as educational qualifications of the individual involved.

The disapproval in no way reflects upon your professional preparation or specific background in the area of clinical psychology. The decision was based primarily on the needs of the department in accord with its profile and qualifications.

This reversal came on the heels of a series of earlier promising developments. While specializing in clinical psychology, Mr. Pittman taught during the preceding academic year, offering courses at Prince George's Community College. Planning to make college teaching his lifetime profession, he had applied for a full time teaching position in the school for the 1972-73 academic year. As the winter proceeded, the chairman of the department described Pittman's chances as "very good." In the spring of 1972, he was referred to as "the leading contender." By summer he was introduced as the man who would be "with us this fall." This seemed natural, since he was selected by the departmental committee from among 30-plus applicants as the department's "No. 1 recommendation."

Pittman's rank of assistant professor and a corresponding salary were approved by the dean of social sciences and the vice president of academic affairs. In July the department chairman asked Pittman for his preferences in the autumn teaching schedule. Mr. and Mrs. Pittman began their search for housing in the area of the college.

And so it went until August 3, when the department chairman broke the news orally that the president and the trustees, at a July 31 meeting, had disapproved Pittman's appointment to the department of psychology. At the same meeting, the trustees and president had also ordered that the two positions open in the department be filled by women, preferably black women. A woman applicant was subsequently hired. At that time, the board and president instructed the department of psychology to fill the remaining position with a black qualified in clinical psychology. In the opinion of the chairman, Pittman would have been hired without difficulty had he been a woman or a black.

This clear case of reverse discrimination has a happy ending. Through the good offices of the opponents of Affirmative Action, the Pittman case received national attention. On November 14, 1972, Pittman was hired by the college with pay retroactive to August 21. On November 15, the president of the college was replaced.

Similar results have been obtained in the area of student recruitment this past year at the University of Massachusetts. The applications of some 300 students were set aside by the admissions department since the students were not members of any favored minority group and the school has an "affirmative action commitment to recruit minority students." Under pressure from outside the campus, the decision was hastily reversed and the 300 applications were reviewed on their individual merits.

Unfortunately such happy endings are all too uncommon in today's academic community. Many educators have been unwilling to take a strong stand. Not only have they acquiesced in the face of Affirmative Action pressures, but in many cases over-anxious administrators have raced beyond even the guidelines placed upon them by

OCR, pushing reverse discrimination to shocking levels. Meanwhile, there has been all too little formal protest from the academic community itself. As of this writing, no group of academic institutions has yet gone to court seeking an injunction against implementation of the Labor Department's Revised Order #4 on the grounds that its enforced discrimination runs directly counter to the 1964 Civil Rights Act. This refusal on the part of most educators to take a strong stand amounts to tacit approval of discrimination on the basis of race and sex and a craven denial of equal opportunity in education.

Confusion on the Campus

This inability or unwillingness to stand on principle has left a wave of confusion and low morale in its wake. Elie Abel, dean of the Columbia Graduate School of Journalism, has agonized in the pages of the *New York Times*, "We can't, in essence, hire, promote, or give a raise to anyone without clearing it over there [HEW]. Are they really trying to tell us we cannot promote our own assistant professors without setting up a nationwide search?"

Educators who feel threatened in the self-determination and internal control of their departments and schools perhaps should also consider the implications which lie behind that threat. When a bureaucrat can threaten withholding virtually millions of dollars in funds from Columbia University, not because Columbia has been found guilty of specific acts of discrimination, but because Co-

lumbia, after a half-dozen attempts and the expenditure of
tens of thousands of dollars in computer studies, has
failed to come up with an Affirmative Action plan satis-
factory to the bureaucracy, the results should be obvious
to all: federal control of higher education now threatens
to produce severe damage to those independent values
which have meant so much for the preservation of our institutions of higher learning and the maintenance of an
open society.

Many of those who have thought themselves most
liberal and most committed to the idea of an open society
which judged each of us on individual merit now find
themselves involved in a process apparently designed to
end any role for individual merit in higher education.
These same educators now so vitally concerned about the
continuance of federal funding for higher education
should recall that their troubles actually began long ago,
at the time when so many colleges and universities accepted the idea of large-scale federal aid for higher education. At that time, some observers warned that federal
aid would ultimately produce government control over
higher education. Anyone familiar with higher education
in the past twenty years knows that those warnings were
dismissed as absurd. Surely the well-intentioned support-
ers of higher education who were making federal funding
available would never consider using that funding as the
basis for control! Or so most American colleges and universities believed a few short years ago.

Today the question of federal encroachment on higher education is no longer a matter of speculation. Affirmative Action has a large and significant role in
determining the future of American higher education. It is
generally considered bad form to say, ''I told you so,''
but even the most casual observer of current Affirmative

Action programming on the campus, as he listens to the aggrieved outcry of so many educators, must be immediately reminded of the biblical warning to those who sow the wind. Few of us would today deny that the whirlwind has arrived.

Who's Discriminating?

The adoption of quotas would be the most radical change one can imagine in the American ethos. The fact that it began to be implemented with no public discussion whatsoever and the fact this change began to be implemented through the activity of bureaucrats is an astonishing feature of the national life at this time.

Norman Podhoretz

ONE OF THE GOALS which most Americans have shared, one of the cornerstones of the American self-assumption, has been that each person should be judged as an individual, on the basis of his own merits. Thus at first glance a program such as Affirmative Action is potentially attractive to many people, since it promises "action" in eliminating discrimination. Most Americans agree that discrimination is wrong when it treats people as members of a group rather than as individuals. However, the question which needs to be raised concerning Affirmative Action is: who is discriminating? Is Affirmative Action the next step in achieving the American dream—or is it a new and particularly vicious form of discrimination?

Quotas or Goals?

In an effort to answer that question, we might profitably examine the definition of Affirmative Action provided by the program's most eloquent spokesman, former head of OCR, Mr. J. Stanley Pottinger:

> The concept of Affirmative Action requires more than mere neutrality on race and sex. It requires the university to determine whether it has failed to recruit, employ, and promote women and minorities commensurate with their availability, even if this failure cannot be traced to specific acts of discrimination by university officials. Where women and minorities are not represented on a university's rolls, despite their availability (that is, where they are "underutilized") the university has an obligation to initiate affirmative efforts to recruit and hire them. The premise of this obligation is that systemic forms of exclusion, inattention, and discrimination cannot be remedied in any meaningful way, in any reasonable length of time, simply by ensuring a future benign neutrality with regard to race and sex. This would perpetuate indefinitely the grossest inequities of past discrimination. Thus there must be some form of positive action, along with a schedule for how such actions are to take place, and an honest appraisal of what the plan is likely to yield—an appraisal that the regulations call a "goal."

Publications of the OCR go on to describe that "goal" and the required method for its achievement: "...the guidelines explicitly require that goals and time-tables be established to eliminate hiring, firing, promotion, recruiting, pay, and fringe benefit discrimination."

The Office of Civil Rights is quick to insist that "goals" are not "quotas." Mr. Pottinger has repeatedly announced that while he favors "goals," he opposes "quotas" which are "rigid" and "arbitrary." In the opinion of Pottinger and OCR, the quota question is nothing more than a rhetorical device in the hands of their critics:

> Every crusade must have its simplistic side—a galvanizing symbol, a bogeyman, a rallying cry. The word "quotas" serves these rhetorical purposes in the present case.

Mr. Pottinger, who served as the architect for much of Affirmative Action before his promotion to the rank of Assistant Attorney General for Civil Rights, makes a valid point when he suggests that quotas *as such* are not required by OCR policy. But it is disingenuous to leave the matter there. It may be that a given policy will result in a quota system without its being called a quota system. This is precisely what has happened in Affirmative Action programming.

Certainly the college and university administrators faced with Affirmative Action have been badly confused in the process. "Goals" and "guidelines" have proven to be nothing more than confusing synonyms for numerical quotas. The college or university faced with proving its innocence by showing "good faith" has discovered that satisfying the bureaucratic task force is a supremely difficult undertaking. Those schools attempting to comply

with Affirmative Action programming find themselves
trapped in a mass of paper work, a labyrinth of bureaucratic guidelines, and an endlessly conflicting collection
of definitions concerning "good faith," "equality,"
"minorities," "goals," and "quotas." A central fact in
the confusion has been the discussion of goals versus
quotas. Endless amounts of ink have been expended on
this semantic distinction. But the distinction remains exclusively semantic.

Professor Paul Seabury of the University of California has been outspoken concerning the artificial nature of
the distinction. In the process, he has developed two hy-
brid labels, which put the question in perspective: the
quoal, a slow-moving quota-goal; and the *gota,* which is
a supple, fast-moving quota-goal.

There is more validity in Professor Seabury's humor
than HEW has been willing to admit. The "re-
sults-oriented goals and timetables" aspect of Affirmative Action simply results in a de facto quota system. As
one highly placed OCR official recently commented:
"The job won't get done unless the university is subject-
ed to specific objectives that are results oriented."

HEW's insistence that it abhors quotas holds little
weight when seen in the light of Mr. J. Stanley Pottinger's remark to the representatives of six Jewish groups.
He said: "While HEW does not endorse quotas, I feel
that HEW has no responsibility to object if quotas are
used by universities on their own initiative." In practice,
the central fact remains that both quotas and goals demand that our colleges and universities treat people as
members of a group rather than as individuals.

Bureaucratic Quotas

The hiring record of the federal bureaucracy is itself a demonstration that the quota principle is approved and enforced, whatever the label. Although the federal government has now issued an order which presumably bars the use of quotas in hiring, the reality is otherwise. Quotas for hiring on the basis of race have existed for years in the Office of Management and Budget, HEW, HUD, the Agriculture Department, and the Labor Department, to name a few instances within the bureaucracy. During the past three years, within the ranks of the Equal Employment Opportunity Commission itself, there have been 85 complaints filed charging reverse discrimination in hiring brought about by a quota system. Since EEOC only has approximately 1,000 employees nationwide, these figures mean that almost 10 percent of the EEOC staff members have filed formal complaint, charging their superiors with discriminatory hiring quotas. This, I remind you, is the state of affairs in the very bureaucratic agency set up to insure no discriminatory hiring. Even since the presumptive federal ban on quotas, the direction of the bureaucracy remains the same. The Department of Justice has recently brought legal pressure to bear which proposes numerical goals for black state policemen in an Alabama case based on the Fourteenth Amendment.

There is little practical difference between saying: (1) "You must aim at a quota of 20 percent Lithuanians on your staff within the next three years," and saying (2) "You must set as your numerical goal recruitment of 20 percent Lithuanians within the next three years." It seems clear that the federal bureaucracy has every intention of enforcing quotas, and no amount of semantic confusion should be allowed to obscure the fact.

Double Standards

Under the guise of non-discrimination, Affirmative Action is actually pursuing a sharply different goal. One of the principal sponsors of that portion of the 1964 Civil Rights Act which has since produced the present situation, Senator Hubert Humphrey, denied that the quota idea would ever result from that legislation. Now, of course, those who have turned to quotas defend their position by asking, "How would social justice otherwise be achieved?" Such advocates of Affirmative Action are thus announcing their willingness to abandon non-discrimination in pursuit of another goal which they deem preferable.

This intention is clearly stated in the bureaucratic guidebook for Affirmative Action, *Questions and Answers for Higher Education Guidelines, Executive Order 11246:*

> There are two basic concepts behind Executive Order 11246: (1) non-discrimination and (2) affirmative action...Non-discrimination requirements of the Executive Order apply to *all* persons. *No* person may be denied employment or related benefits on grounds of race, color, religion, sex and national origin. Affirmative Action requirements are designed to further employment opportunity for women, and minorities who are defined as Negroes, Spanish-surnamed, American Indians, and Orientals.

Remember that the original executive order insisted that affirmative action was to be taken to guarantee equal treatment without regard to race, color, religion, sex or national origin. HEW, however, insists that Affirmative Action involves not equal treatment, but special efforts to recruit, employ, and promote some persons on the basis of race, sex, or national origin. Equal treatment is no longer the measure of compliance—proper "utilization" of women or minorities is to be the guideline. In practical terms this means that a college or university is required to make statistical analysis of its work force on the basis of sex and race. If "deficiencies" can be detected in the number of women or selected minority members employed, the university is then expected to establish numerical goals and take "affirmative action" to correct its statistical discrimination.

In other words, everyone is equal, but some are more equal than others. Discrimination is unacceptable, except when the bureaucracy orders schools to discriminate.

Group Privilege versus Individual Merit

At the heart of this matter lies a fundamental question concerning group rights vs. individual rights. The HEW directives which now attempt enforcement of group proportional rights are pushing toward a major change in this nation's traditional conception of equality and opportunity. Affirmative Action, which evolved from an attempt to end discriminatory practices, has now been elevated to the level of an ideology in its own right. The means has become the end. The bureaucracy which pressed Affirmative Action upon the academic community does so in the apparent assurance that discrimination is the means to achieve true equality. Individual merit is to be set aside in favor of a new, collective goal for the social order.

Reverse discrimination has been the direct and inevitable result. A quota, goal, guideline, or whatever, which enforces hiring preferences according to sex or race, can do so only by denying otherwise qualified candidates proper consideration for the same position. Affirmative Action quotas are by nature inflexible. Such quotas can achieve their announced end only by enforcing the very discrimination they once set out to stop.

Perhaps in this sense Affirmative Action is an ideal example of what can happen when ideology runs amok. To draw a parallel, the civil rights movement of the 1960s shared the same concern for minorities, and was aimed at ending discrimination. After passage of the Civil Rights Act, however, it soon became clear that equal opportunity, though enforced by law, did not necessarily end all discrimination. Cultural barriers were also involved; overcoming them takes time.

And it was precisely time that some ideologues were unwilling to grant. Results had to come and come quickly—thus Affirmative Action was born. It is an interesting historical footnote that the ideological lust for quick results converted the quest for non-discrimination of the 1960s into the reverse discrimination of the 1970s.

Academic Impact

Nowhere have the results of Affirmative Action been more disappointing and damaging than in the field of higher education. In the earlier stages of Affirmative Action, it was not yet clear to many people within the academy what the program involved or how far-reaching its effects would be. Many professors, secure in their own position by reputation or tenure, have only recently begun to appreciate the hiring difficulties of many schools and qualified scholars. Most of those same professors have long recognized that blacks, members of other minority groups, and women have been denied various opportunities without proper regard to their qualifications. Those professors greeted with approval the federal civil rights acts of the mid-sixties and the executive order banning further discrimination. They looked forward to the day when all individuals would be judged on the basis of their abilities, not on the basis of their sex, race, or group membership.

By the early seventies, many of these professors were facing a painful disappointment. The news was beginning to circulate that the programs presumably devised to fight the old discriminations were now introducing wholesale discriminations of their own. In the name of public policy designed to remove discrimination from the academic community, the thrust of HEW Affirmative Action programs seemed to be demanding the deliberate introduction of discriminatory quotas. Affirmative Action, through a mixture of idealism, excess zeal, and political authority, seemed to be destroying precisely those values which it had been brought into existence to protect. Equality of opportunity had been increasingly set aside in favor of equality of result, thus denying the whole basis of professional qualification or individual achievement.

The new programs were treating people as members of groups rather than as individuals, and the reaction within the academic community began to be increasingly critical. Columbia University philosophy professor Charles Frankel fumed, "We haven't had this kind of in-

tervention since the days of Joe McCarthy.'' John Bun-
zel, president of California State College at San Jose,
agreed: ''I've heard cases of people hiring someone just
to avoid a hassle with the federal government. I know of
people who have gotten letters saying, 'Your qualifications are excellent but we are looking for a black or a
woman this year.' ''

In the past two years increasing numbers of announcements for job opportunities within the academic
community have appeared in professional journals and
other academic outlets, making specific reference to race,
sex, or ethnic background of the prospective applicant,
usually in such a way as to suggest that such applicants
will receive preferential treatment. The pressures for such
preferential hiring are now an accepted fact in the American academic community.

In an effort to resist such pressures and force a reex-
amination of the entire underlying issue, several groups
of scholars have made a determined effort to accumulate
information of such abuses. These defenders of academic
freedom and individual merit have been sufficiently successful in stating their case that an ombudsman has now
been appointed by the Department of Health, Education,
and Welfare to examine all complaints of reverse discrimination. Samuel H. Solomon, special assistant to the Office of Civil Rights, has already investigated some
seventy cases and has discovered that a number of America's colleges and universities are engaging in reverse discrimination favoring women and minority candidates for
faculty and staff jobs over equally qualified or better
qualified white males. Solomon himself has commented,
''I've been out on the campus trail in recent weeks and I
am getting the impression that most of the institutions are
engaging in some form of discrimination against white

males.'' He also detected what he described as ill-advised recruiting practices, in which schools advertising faculty and staff positions identify them as ''affirmative action positions''—which according to Solomon has become ''a code phrase for minorities or women only.'' In the face of this pressure, HEW and other government agencies have been at pains to issue new ''guidelines'' and ''clarifications'' designed to stop such malpractices. Yet there seems little or no indication that the thrust of Affirmative Action has been turned from its original channel. In fact, the pressures for Affirmative Action compliance seem greater than ever.

The result is a rush of academic hiring practices based upon race and sex. It would require another book to publish the letters of inquiry, faculty minutes, questionnaires, and lists of available positions which have accumulated in past months, all reflecting such discriminatory hiring practices.

Several forms of damage have resulted. In the first place, quality and quotas simply do not go together. In the assault on academic quality which necessarily accompanies the imposition of minority quotas, the Jewish community has had most to lose because of its high concentration of students and professors in higher education. Jews make up some 3 percent of the general population, but a far higher percentage of the academy, including many of its most highly qualified members. Fortunately, something of the Jewish sense of humor has been retained in the face of this threat. Recently a spokesman for the Jewish Defense League commented with tongue in cheek:

> Jews come from athletically deprived backgrounds. Irving is kept off the sandlot by too much homework and too many music lessons. He is now 25 and still can't play

ball, but "he has the desire to learn." Therefore, the
Jewish Defense League is demanding that New York City
which has a 24 percent Jewish population, fill the city's
ball teams with 24 percent Jews.

When we consider what this would do to baseball in
New York, our reaction is a chuckle. When we consider
what a similar approach in admissions and faculty hiring
is doing to American higher education, the matter is a
good deal less entertaining.

Another form of the erosion of quality that Affirmative Action has brought to higher education is the strongly anti-intellectual tone the program has generated. Today
on many campuses there seems less interest in a genuine
life of the mind than in something that might be termed
the "new pluralism." The new pluralism is based upon
the assumption that the campus is fair game for whatever
the various special interest groups may choose to demand. Any unwillingness to accept courses in free love,
advanced bongo drum programs, majors in homosexuali-
ty, or any of the other numerous and kinky demands
made today in the name of the new pluralism, is usually
put down to racism and sexism.

Today everyone wants greater representation on faculties, open admissions, funding for special programs—in
short, everyone wants a share of the already painfully
limited academic resources. Any plea that standards and
quality must be maintained is treated as an affront to the
principles of participatory democracy.

These principles are coming to faculties now in the
Affirmative Action assumption that racial and sexual faculty proportions should be identical to the racial and sexual proportions of society as a whole. Attaining such
racial and sexual proportions is a practical impossibility.
For example, there simply are not enough academically

trained women to staff 50 percent of America's institutions of higher learning, though this fact does not deter the attempt. Nor does any concern over finding academically qualified persons in such large numbers seem to dismay the ideologues. Sacramento State College has sent out letters announcing, "Sacramento State College is currently engaged in an Affirmative Action Program, the goal of which is to recruit, hire, and promote ethnic and women candidates until they comprise the same proportion of the faculty as they do of the general population."

The practical reality is, the enforcement of minority quotas on faculties is lowering professional and academic standards. The further Affirmative Action inflicts its ideology of statistics on the universities, the less they will be able to call themselves institutes of higher education.

What is a Minority?

A proper Sociological Caucus should contain: two blacks (one man, one woman); one Chicano (or Chicana on alternate elections); one person to be, in alphabetical rotation, Amerindian, Asian, and Eskimo; and sixteen white Anglos. Of the latter, eight will have to be men and eight women; fourteen will have to be heterosexual and two homosexual (one of these to be a lesbian); one Jewish, ten Protestant, four Roman Catholic; and one, in alphabetical rotation, Buddhist, Mormon and Muslim; fifteen will have to be sighted and one blind; eight must be juvenile, four mature and four senile; and two must be intelligent, ten mediocre, and four stupid.

Pierre L. van den Berghe

T HE WORD "minority" does not appear so much as once in either Executive Order 11246 or in the 1964 Civil Rights Act. Yet in Labor Department Revised Order #4, the key enabling document of Affirmative Action, the word "minority" is used in one form or another 65 times, but is never defined. "The Higher Education Guidelines" issued by HEW in connection with its Affirmative Action program does provide a definition of sorts, including in that category "Negroes, Spanish-surnamed, American Indians, and Orientals...."

Since neither the original civil rights legislation nor the related executive order ever mentioned the word, thus reserving "minorities" for later Affirmative Action guidelines, the question naturally arises: Where did the Affirmative Action zealots get their definition of the word? The answer is frightening, especially for those interested in the future of higher education.

The OCR has admitted borrowing its working definition of "minority" from the Department of Labor, one first used at the time the "Philadelphia Plan" was implemented. The Department of Labor had developed a definition of "minority" which, correctly or not, was felt to be appropriate to hiring patterns in the construction industry. It was this definition that OCR borrowed to apply across the board in developing Affirmative Action plans for higher education. However surprising this may be to the Washington mentality, it is likely that there *are* differences between the construction industry and higher education. These might well include differing patterns of discrimination, not to mention differing patterns of job performance.

We probably need not be unduly concerned about the deficiencies in the OCR definition of "minorities" in higher education. The list of minorities is likely to grow very rapidly. As more and more groups discover the special privileges that can accrue to officially recognized "disadvantaged" minorities, colleges and universities will probably find themselves called upon to extend hiring quotas even further. As Senator James Buckley (Conservative-Republican, New York) told his colleagues, "And so our colleges and universities will find themselves forced to punch into their computer cards more and more categories of human beings so that they may achieve the exact mix of sex, race, religion, and national origin that will be required to satisfy their ever more fastidious inquisitors.''

Pressures for Compliance

Certainly great pressure has already developed to compel the measurement of ''minorities.'' Many administrators have simply abandoned any attempt to resist that pressure. Few academics are anxious to appear in opposition to a program which purports to end discrimination. Even fewer are willing to jeopardize federal funding for their institutions. Brooklyn College, in direct violation of New York State law, has twice asked its faculty and staff to fill out detailed questionnaires which deal directly with individual race and ethnic background. In his covering letter, the school's president urged faculty and staff to provide the information since ''...considerable sums which the university receives from the federal government are in jeopardy.... At this stage of the game, we have no choice but to perform this task as quickly and expeditiously as possible.''

The same rush to conform to political pressures has also begun to occur in racial measurement of student bodies. Following a campus strike, President Robben Fleming of the University of Michigan caved in to demands for 10 percent black enrollment goals. Outraged faculty warned that present black attrition rates were running close to 50 percent at the university and that any attempt to triple the number of blacks (now about 3.5 percent of total enrollment) could be achieved only by

lowering standards and thus sending the attrition rate even
higher. Nevertheless, the University of Michigan has now
accepted racial quotas for student enrollment.

As we move toward a period in which we measure
faculty, students and academic standards by racial and
sexual quotas, it is worth remembering that to date no
comprehensive, statistically valid study has yet become
available which demonstrates conclusively either the existence or the degree of discrimination in academic employment. In other words, even if we accept the vicious
premise that faculty or students should be measured not
by ability but by race or sex, we are still confronted with
the problem of deciding which "minorities" should receive this special privilege.

What Is a Protected Class?

Though it is fashionable today to discuss "oppressed
minorities," the practical problem of identifying and dis-
tinguishing those minorities is very great. Dr. Aaron Wil-
davsky, dean of the Graduate School of Public Policy at
the Berkeley campus of the University of California, has
totaled all the currently fashionable "oppressed minorities" and concluded that the nation is composed of "374
percent minorities." In the same spirit, a departmental
chairman of a large Eastern university has posted the
qualifications for a new faculty member: a woman Egyp-
tologist, black, with a Spanish surname, born on a South-
western Indian reservation.

Even if we were to grant that some categories of faculty or students should receive special academic privilege,
how do we decide which categories should be selected?

Columbia University lists four protected classes: Black-Negro, Oriental, American Indian, Spanish-surnamed American. Brooklyn College originally listed five: American Indian, Black, Indian (Asian), Oriental, and Puerto Rican. Three months later, Indian (Asian) was dropped from the list and replaced by Italian-American. In the San Francisco area there seem to be seven groups singled out for special attention: Negro/Black, Chinese, Japanese, Korean, American Indian, Filipino, Spanish-speaking/Spanish-surname. Apparently definition of a protected class is subject to geography and institutional whim.

In practice, such categories quickly reach absurdity:

— Though a higher percentage of blacks than whites are poor, there are rich blacks; should the government insist that sons of well-to-do blacks not receive preferential treatment?

— If the Spanish surname in question is Patino (former Bolivian tin mine owners), should preferential treatment be granted?

— Why include Chinese and Japanese as protected groups when the Japanese have a high rate of financial accomplishment and the Chinese have the highest per capita rate of Ph.D.'s in the country?

— If race is the standard for identifying an oppressed group, what about Appalachian whites?

As we select our oppressed minorities who are "underutilized" in higher education, we might remember that not only blacks, but also Irish, Greeks, Italians, Poles and all other Slavs (including Czechs, Croations, Slovenes, Slovaks and Serbs) are underrepresented.

Perhaps we should also consider religious underutilization. Catholics comprise 30 percent of the population, but occupy a far smaller percentage of higher educational posts. As author, professor, and scholar Russell Kirk recently asked:

When will Harvard make a Dominican its president—a black Dominican, say? When will Brandeis appoint half a dozen nuns to professorial chairs? How many deans at the University of Texas are Mexican-American and Papist and maternal?

Many institutions of the learning allegedly higher already have converted themselves into theaters of the absurd. Why shouldn't we go whole hog?

Indeed, why not go whole hog? The State University at Purchase, New York, has been formally charged with discrimination against Italian-Americans. In a complaint filed with the state Human Rights Division, the Westchester County Federation of Italian American Organizations has charged the school with failure to offer Italian language courses or hire Italian faculty and administrators. The chairman of the federation, Mr. Raphael Riverso, has announced, "Since the population of Westchester County is 40 to 50 percent Italian, we are demanding that the university begin a program to hire qualified Italians until they make up 40 percent of the supervisory, teaching and administrative staff."

Once the process is begun, once we grant special privilege to "oppressed minorities," the inevitable tendency will be toward an endless proliferation of oppressed minorities. If race or sex are suitable bases for determining special privilege, why not include groups with special physical characteristics? Professor Murray Rothbard recently took a humorous view of the prospect:

> And how about a group in which I have a certain personal interest—short people? May we not maintain that "shorts" are the first to be fired and the last to be hired: and where in blazes are the short executives, the short bankers, the short senators, and presidents? There is surely no genetic evidence to prove that short people are inferior to talls (look at Napoleon). Shall we not call

upon short pride, short institutes, short history courses; shall we not demand short quotas everywhere? Women have notoriously discriminated in favor of talls over shorts, and in how many movies have shorts—openly displayed as such—played the romantic leads? Professor Saul D. Feldman, a short sociologist at Case-Western Reserve, has now quantified some of this short-oppression...and also points out the subtle corruption of our language (presumably as engineered by a tall-conspiracy); for people are described as "short-sighted, short-changed, short-circuited, and short in cash."

The whole idea of quotas, oppressed minorities and measurement by group rather than individual standards is ludicrous, nowhere more so than in the academic community. But as the laughter dies down, we might recall one painful and inescapable fact: it is impossible to achieve a quota for one group without reducing the "quota" for another. By pursuing justice too zealously, we are fostering an injustice.

The Problem of Measurement

Even after we have decided whom to reward and whom to punish, we are still faced with a problem: How do we gather information to measure quotas for various minorities?

There are a number of state and local laws specifically forbidding the requirement of racial, sexual, religious or ethnic information as a condition of employment. Presumably, all this is now set aside. *Questions and Answers for Higher Education Guidelines* states:

Under the principle of federal supremacy, requirements
for information under the executive order supersede any
conflicting state or local law. An individual, however, is
not legally bound to report such information about himself.

The real problem lies in the fact that the institutions
involved are required to provide that information under
Affirmative Action, *whether or not the individual employees are willing to cooperate.* Columbia University
conducted its inquiry into such matters in a way which
would give the necessary A.A. information and still not
involve individual faculty. "Census reporters" were appointed in each division of the school. These reporters
were to make ethnic identifications "based upon the re-
porter's general knowledge and observation of the em-
ployee." Applicants for new positions (HEW requires
that all applicants be classified, whether or not subsequently employed) were to be checked out by "visual
survey." All of this was to take place without the knowledge of the individuals being "surveyed." This is ridicu-
lous. It is hard enough, in some cases, to tell an
individual's sex at a glance, much less ancestry or oppressed status. A few short years ago, had a novel described such a system of ethnic measurement at some
fictitious university, it would have been received as a
farce or a fantasy. Today such antics are undertaken as a
serious enterprise.

Those institutions more open in their measurement
techniques have also had their problems. A sociologist at
Syracuse University, attempting to gather information on
the status of black professors in predominantly white
schools, quickly discovered the reason: many of those
contacted in his national survey simply refused to cooperate. A number of the faculty members labeled black by
the sociologist's informants returned their questionnaires

with "white" indicated as their racial preference. Other professors wrote, asking for more information:

> I would request you kindly to define more precisely what you mean by the term "black"? Am I right in supposing that you are seeking information regarding American faculty of African descent? Or do you wish West Indian and African faculty members to be included—or dark skinned faculty from other countries?

Michigan State University has also had its problems in computing minorities. Robert Perrin, vice president for university relations, has described what he calls "the numbers game," a game involving collection of vast amounts of statistical data concerning the employees and students of a school. He bemoans the lack of cooperation among those persons being counted. For example, some 150 MSU students categorized themselves as American Indians, fifteen times the actual number on campus. Others returned cards with additional categories marked: "Super Jew," "Texan," "50th Generation Hun," or "female." As Perrin describes the result, "One determined iconoclast not only mutilated and spindled his computer card, he stapled it as well."

Are We Helping or Hurting?

Meanwhile, what effect does Affirmative Action have upon the minorities we are trying to help? Here the story is saddest of all.

One of the casualties of Affirmative Action has been the black college and university. Competition has become so intense for qualified black professors that the black schools are losing their most qualified faculty members to those large, prosperous, predominantly white institutions that can afford to pay substantially higher salaries.

Meanwhile, qualified minority members are also penalized by Affirmative Action. What quotas and special privileges are saying all too clearly is that the minority member just doesn't have what it takes and as the result must be given what he is unqualified to earn. Even the minority member who earns his competence will surely be undermined as the result. The suspicion will be present in his mind and everyone else's that his success may be due to special privilege, not talent and hard work. No one resents this aspect of Affirmative Action more bitterly than the qualified minority member himself.

One of those highly qualified blacks is Professor Thomas Sowell of the University of California of Los Angeles, now on leave at the Urban Institute in Washington, D.C. In response to what has become known as an "Affirmative Action letter," Sowell stated his case plainly:

> September 18, 1972
> Professor Frank C. Pierson
> Chairman
> Department of Economics
> Swarthmore College
> Swarthmore, Pennsylvania
>
> Dear Professor Pierson:
>
> This morning I was pleased to receive a letter from Swarthmore College, an institution for which I have long had respect, and reports from which have added to my admiration.
>
> Then I opened the letter and learned that "Swarthmore College is actively looking for a black economist...." and the phrase that came immediately to mind was one from a bygone era, when a very different kind of emo-

tionalism was abroad, and a counsel facing Senator Joseph McCarthy said, "Sir, have you no shame?"

What purpose is to be served by this sort of thing? Surely a labor economist of your reputation must know that unemployment among black Ph.D.'s is one of the least of our social problems, and has been for many years—long before "affirmative action." In general, even, the salary is no higher at a top college than at less prestigious institutions for a given individual. So you are doing very little for black faculty members with broadcast recruiting campaigns like this (I note the letter is mimeographed). Maybe you think you are doing something for race relations. If you are going to find a Swarthmore-quality black faculty member, that is one thing. But Swarthmore-quality faculty members are found through Swarthmore-quality channels and not through mimeographed letters of this sort. *Many a self-respecting black scholar would never accept an offer like this,* even if he might otherwise enjoy teaching at Swarthmore. When Bill Allen was department chairman at UCLA he violently refused to hire anyone on the basis of ethnic representation—and thereby made it possible for me to come there a year later with my head held up. Your approach tends to *make the job unattractive to anyone who regards himself as a scholar or a man,* and *thereby throws it open to opportunists.*

Despite all the brave talk in academia about "affirmative action" without lowering quality standards, you and I both know that it takes many years to create a qualified faculty member of any color, and no increased demand is going to increase the supply immediately *unless* you lower quality. Now what good is going to come from lower standards that will make "black" equivalent to "substandard" in the eyes of black and white students alike? Can you imagine that this is going to *reduce* racism? On the contrary, more and more thoughtful people are beginning to worry that the next generation will see an increasing amount of bigotry among those whites educated at some of the most liberal institutions, where this is the picture that is presented to them, however noble the rhetoric that accompanies it.

You and I both know that many of *these "special" re-cruiting efforts are not aimed at helping black faculty members or black or white students, but rather at hanging onto the school's federal money.* Now, I have nothing against money. I have not been so familiar with it as to have contempt for it. But there are limits to what should be done to get it, and particularly so for an institution with a proud tradition, at a time when the government it-self is wavering and having second thoughts about this policy, and when just a little courage from a few men in "responsible" positions might make a difference.

Yours sincerely,

(s) Thomas Sowell

Professor Sowell has ample reason for his anger. A young black woman with an I.Q. of 142 and comparable grades and recommendations was told by a national or-ganization that she would be eligible to receive financial aid for legal studies if her scores were low enough. The scores were *too high;* the aid was denied. Another young black applied for a well-publicized doctoral fellowship specifically for black students. The fellowship was denied to this student, despite his brilliant academic record, be-cause his social and political views were insufficiently militant. The current thrust toward "helping" the minori-ty member in pursuit of his education seems determined to penalize real achievement wherever it appears.

Meanwhile, the unqualified minority member is also cheated in the education which Affirmative Action prom-ises. In the early 1960s, a great drive was under way to bring minority students to predominantly white schools. Between 1964 and 1970, the number of blacks on previ-ously white campuses jumped 173 percent, from 114,000 to 310,000. The promise held out to a generation of young blacks was a lifetime of material success within "the system," a promise which higher education could not hope to deliver, especially since many of those minority students attracted to the campus were unprepared for the life and work which was thrust upon them.

Just as many of these students are ill-prepared to participate in higher education, so are many of their professors ill-prepared to offer a quality experience to their students. Affirmative Action has greatly aggravated this tendency. The attempt to achieve a statistically adequate representation of women and ethnic groups on college faculties has tended to produce a rush to discover sufficient numbers of well-qualified professors with minority credentials. In actual practice, the numbers demanded of such minority types far exceed the qualified people available. Thus a strange new word has entered the Affirmative Action dialogue. Today we talk about the appointment of persons who are not qualified, but who are "qualifiable." In point of fact, the guidelines state: "Neither minority nor female employees should be required to possess higher qualifications than those of the lowest qualified incumbent."

Has merit come to mean only equality on the lowest level of performance? Not only does this do an injustice to the institution and the students coming in contact with faculty members unqualified to hold their position, but also it excludes from consideration large numbers of an entire generation of young scholars, quite well-qualified to hold a position, yet often rendered ineligible by virtue of their nonmembership in an HEW-approved minority group. Unfair discrimination and the lowering of standards go far beyond reverse discrimination. Today even well-qualified blacks are passed over for consideration—because they are not from the ghetto. The search is not merely for blacks, but for "authentic ghetto types."

Black professors and black students alike have been downgraded. The first-rank performers have suffered this downgrading because whatever accomplishment they attain is often assumed to be the result of special privilege. Meanwhile, unqualified professors and students from various ethnic groups have been cheated into assuming that they were taking their place in a true educational framework, when, in fact, all the standards which gave the framework any meaning have been undercut. As one Cornell professor bluntly put it: "I give them all A's and B's, and to hell with them." Surely this is not the "equality" which we desire for higher education.

Such distortions are themselves the product of paternalistic recruiting quotas for minorities. Again to quote Professor Sowell:

> Most people are unaware of the extent to which the severe educational problems of black college students are functions of the manner in which they are recruited and selected, rather than simply being the inevitable result of "cultural deprivation." There is no question that the overwhelming bulk of black youth have been given grossly inadequate preparation in the public schools. However, the overwhelming bulk of black youth do not go on to college, and while the proportion of these youth who are educationally well prepared for college is very low, in absolute numbers there are literally tens of thousands of them who are, by all the usual indices—far too many for the top universities to be forced to have as many inadequately prepared black students as they do. The fact that standardized examinations may be less reliable for ethnic minorities than for others have been used as a blanket excuse for recruiting and selecting black students on all sorts of nonintellectual criteria, from the ideological to the whimsical. Programs for black people tend to attract more than their fair share of vague humanitarians and socio-political doctrinaires seeking to implement some special vision. Not all are as obtuse as the special admissions committee for black students at one Ivy League university who objected to admitting three black applicants with College Board scores in the 700's on grounds that they were probably—God forbid—middle

class, and that there were other blacks applying who were more "interesting" cases—but this general kind of thinking is by no means rare. One consequence of this is that, despite the buzz of recruiting activity, there are many black students who belong in the best colleges in the country who have not been reached with the information and financial aid offers that would bring them there, and are languishing at some of the worst colleges in the country. At the same time other black students are in over their heads at the top colleges, struggling—or being maneuvered—toward a degree.

Plainly, the black students themselves have been the principal casualty of the system. The reaction is often a wave of anti-intellectualism and an orientation toward nonachievement, accompanied by a thirst for "relevance" and "black studies." How can we expect anything but racial antagonism and the posturing of black separatism when we have so effectively insured that genuine academic achievement is usually closed to the blacks in our colleges and universities? The situation cries out to recruit and educate young people, black or white, on the basis of their individual ability. Yet this is exactly what Affirmative Action and the patronizing zealotry lying behind it will not permit.

Overcoming Discrimination

Racial and ethnic forms of social engineering are always risky business. Witness the results of a century-long social experiment which treated the American Indian as a member of a "protected class" and ward of the federal bureaucracy. Yet something can be done to alleviate dis-

crimination. The Jews have done just that in America.
Long denied a place in the academic community, or
granted only a small maximum quota, the Jews have
carved a place for themselves through ability and effort
until today they hold a major position on the American
campus. This did not come about through government in-
tervention or quotas favoring Jews. It was possible only
because we enjoyed a system which recognized individual
ability and emphasized individual achievement.

How About Women?

I envy the young and the young in heart, who do not experience my occasional difficulties in grasping that while American women, who are more than 50 percent, are a minority, American Jews, who are fewer than 3 percent, are not a minority.

Milton Himmelfarb

MANY OF US would agree with such a common sense view. Most Americans, men and women alike, would perhaps go even further, regarding themselves primarily as individuals rather than members of some racial, ethnic, religious, sexual, intellectual, or economic group. They would probably agree that, sociology notwithstanding, there are no such things as "group rights." Only individuals have rights and only individuals can be discriminated against.

Still, when we discuss the question of discrimination

and Affirmative Action programming, we should remember that the single largest category of all the "minorities" under discussion is women. Most of the problems which · apply to other A.A. programs apply with special force to women.

We also should remember that valid complaints do exist. There can be no question that women do not always receive equal treatment. Top starting salaries for men and women of equal qualification in the same profession are usually not equal. Employment opportunities are frequently not equal even in areas where little or no difference exists between men and women in their capacity to do the job.

The academic community is one of those areas. There are evidences that women, for whatever reason, have usually been less valued members of the academic community than their male counterparts. Women are still paid less as full time college and university faculty members. Women comprise some 22 percent of faculty and receive salaries on the average approximately $2,500 less than men. Undoubtedly there have been in the past, and still are at present, instances in which women of equal or superior qualification did not have an opportunity to equal pay for the same work or for a particular promotion which went instead to a man of perhaps inferior qualification. There are famous universities which have never chosen a woman as chairman of a department. On many campuses women teachers tend to be engaged to handle overload problems in undergraduate survey courses. Yes, there are reasons for valid complaint concerning unequal treatment.

Times Are Changing

Throughout society today, however, many positions formerly reserved for men are now attracting a growing number of women. Positions ranging from police officer to bank manager to truck driver are now more likely to be filled with women. Though only about 18 percent of managerial positions are currently occupied by women, the figure continues to rise and each year more coeds are being interviewed for jobs with management potential. Even the unions are faced with growing pressure for providing women a larger role, not only for promotion in industrial plants but also for a larger role in union leadership.

A higher percentage of total college enrollment is now filled with women. This is due in part to the removal of draft pressures, which has caused a decline in male enrollment. But many of those women now returning to school have been those who married young and who are now seeking the education which circumstances earlier denied.

Similarly, though naturally in far smaller numbers, women are taking a greater interest in joining college faculties. But it should be remembered, even by the most insistent partisan of equal rights for women, that most college and university teaching situations involve certain factors, common to the lives of many if not most women, that have a bearing on salaries and promotion. As a group, women have been less likely to complete terminal degrees, thus reducing their value in academic positions. As a group, women are far more likely to be affected in their careers by marriage and children, thus in some cases ending their desire for further education or for a continua-

tion of their teaching position. Thus the tenure and qualification of many women are frequently less than those of
their male counterparts. For those women who indeed
have equal or superior credentials, equality of opportunity
for various positions should certainly be available to
them, but it would be incorrect to assume that the most
pressing concern in the lives of all the women in the
country is a desire to be a college professor or take a
Ph.D.

Despite these factors, sharp gains have occurred in
the number of earned doctorates for women. In a number
of disciplines, especially in the social sciences, the number of women receiving terminal degrees has risen substantially faster than men since the mid-1960s. Even in
those disciplines where the greatest growth of women's
Ph.D.'s has occurred, however, women still account for
only approximately 12 percent to 24 percent of the total
degrees granted.

The Egalitarian Thrust of the Age

The same highly politicized lust for group-oriented
"equality" which plagues other portions of Affirmative
Action also is present in so-called women's liberation.
Here again the political history goes back to the 1964
Civil Rights Act. The Southern attempt to obstruct the
bill was failing, and Howard Smith, the "Virginia swamp
fox" of the House Rules Committee, was casting about
for a last-minute amendment which might make the
whole project politically unpalatable to its Northern sup-

porters, so unpalatable that the bill would not pass. The amendment which he succeeded in attaching to the bill was an inclusion of women as an object of federal protection in employment. Sex was added to race, religion, and national origin as illegal grounds for hiring discrimination. Much to the surprise of the chivalrous Congressman Smith, the bill passed, amendment and all.

What neither Howard Smith nor anyone else might have guessed was that a decade later the Office of Civil Rights would seize sexism as the most convenient means of bringing the campuses to heel. In the face of all the difficulties involved in measuring ethnic quotas and identifying minorities, sex appears to be a wonderfully simple and easily quantifiable factor for the enforcement of quotas. Outspoken advocates of women's liberation have not been slow to sense the direction of OCR thinking. We are now seeing sex as the rising egalitarian issue on campus.

In a time of tightened budgets and little hiring, those schools most deeply involved in A.A. compliance may soon be hiring only women, pushing blacks and other minorities entirely out of the picture. At least some 350 class action complaints were already filed by women on college campuses in the early months of 1973. The pressures have grown intense. Even Stanley Pottinger was considered to be an insufficiently aggressive champion for the cause of women's rights. Pottinger's promotion to assistant attorney general was opposed on that ground by the League of Academic Women.

One of the pressures thus generated is not merely for equality in hiring or pay, but is a demand for back pay and damages to make up for alleged prior inequality. Precedents already exist in the business world, where American Telephone and Telegraph, among others, have agreed to pay reparations to women.

The National Organization of Women and the American Nurses Association have filed complaints against several universities with the Equal Employment Opportunity Commission, on the grounds that the schools' retirement plans discriminate against women. The defense insists, of course, that women on the average *do live longer,* thus explaining the difference in the actuarial tables. Whether or not the courts will give legal recognition to this difference between the sexes remains to be seen.

Federal involvement in the area of sex discrimination also continues to expand. The U.S. Commission on Civil Rights, the monitoring agency for all antidiscrimination legislation, has now been empowered to investigate discrimination based on sex. The growing federal interest in sex discrimination, coupled with the current tendency toward litigation as a weapon for forcing various highly political issues, promises to have a large impact throughout society, an impact of particular importance for colleges and universities.

For example, the Equal Pay Act, as enforced by the Department of Labor, is a powerful weapon in forcing compliance. Complaint may be made against an employer by telephone or anonymous tip. No documentation is required. In a recent report in *The Chronicle of Higher Education*, Ms. Bernice Sandler, director of the Project on the Status and Education of Women for the Association of American Colleges, outlined the process with considerable relish:

> Any person—employee or not—can look in the telephone directory for the phone number of the nearest regional office of the Wage and Hour Division, the Department of Labor, and report one's suspicion that there is a violation of the Equal Pay Act at X institution. A particular department or occupational classification or individual can be specified; no documentation is required. The identity of a

complainant or person furnishing information is never revealed without that person's knowledge and consent.

An employer often does not know that someone has called the Wage and Hour Division. Under the act, the government has the power to conduct routine reviews, whether or not a complaint has been reported.

A woman might call, stating that she suspects she is being underpaid in the English department. Within a few weeks, a compliance officer will appear at the institution to do a "routine check." The investigator can review the entire establishment or may choose to limit the review to a few departments, apparently chosen at random but obviously including the English department.

If a violation is found, the employer is asked to settle on the spot: to raise the salaries of the underpaid persons and to give back pay.

It would be hard to imagine a more clear-cut exercise of raw administrative power, with wide latitude for discretion concerning what is or is not a violation, and with virtually no guarantees or legal safeguards provided for the employer. Of course it might be argued that the employer can always appeal the decision in court, *if* he can afford the heavy costs and endless delays of litigation.

The women's rights movement moves rapidly on other fronts as well. Michigan State University has accepted the recommendations of the MSU Women's Steering Committee, authorizing salary adjustments of $118,658 to 138 women faculty members, establishing a Women's Advisory Council, establishing the position of director of women's athletics, and allowing women to compete on an equal basis for positions in the previously all-male MSU marching band.

Women activists occupied the central switchboard offices of Boston State College for fifty-two hours, leaving only after administrators promised cooperation in establishing space for a child-care facility, equalization of

athletic expenditures for men and women, and establishment of a women's study curriculum.

The Women's Law Association at Harvard Law
School has asked for a federal investigation of possible
discrimination against women in hiring, admission, and
recruitment, plus whatever other action may be required
to eliminate discriminatory practices. And so it goes with
women's rights on the campus front these days.

Impact on Colleges and Universities

As in the case of minority quotas, serious confusions
and potential injustices are involved in academic quotas
for women. How does a school determine that women are
"underutilized"? The current recommended bureaucratic
method is to measure the percentage of degrees granted
nationally to women in a particular discipline against the
percentage of total teaching positions held by women in
that same discipline on a particular campus. Never mind
whether those women available nationally wish to teach
at your school; never mind whether you have positions
available to offer those women; above all, never mind
whether or not those women candidates interviewed for a
job are the best qualified for the particular job in the
opinion of faculty and administration. No, the only deciding factor is to be the quota.

And the quota for hiring women is in process of upward revision. Those zealots who think in quantities rather than personalities have decided that an insufficient
number of women are entering academic life. Why not
have as many women as men completing terminal degrees

and assuming teaching positions? Why not indeed, unless women, for whatever reason peculiar to their individual taste and judgment, would prefer to do something else!

In an effort to force upward revision of the academic quotas for women, Title IX of the 1972 Higher Education Act contains provisions prohibiting sex discrimination in all federally assisted educational programs. Under special scrutiny are institutions of professional and graduate education. HEW has yet to formulate complete guidelines for the project, but it seems clear that graduate schools will soon be required to establish sex quotas for admissions and for numbers of graduates. One such program already contemplated by a Western university has been described in the following terms:

> The university would be charged with the responsibility of conducting an analysis of its students to determine where women are underrepresented, setting reasonable goals and timetables for correcting underrepresentation and designing a program through which it would achieve these goals. Appropriate steps to take under this procedure would include: a review of admission procedures; the selection of admission committee members on the basis of their ability to be impartial with regard to the admission of women; a review of financial aid distribution; the development of affirmative recruiting techniques; and the integration of courses concerning women into the curriculum.

Frenzied Overreaction

It seems clear that in the case of women, as in the case of minorities, individual achievement is to be replaced with Affirmative Action quotas and group pressures. Unfortunately, there has been a frenzied rush to compliance which offers little or no leadership on behalf of the concept of individual measurement, for men or women.

The secretary of education for the Commonwealth of Pennsylvania has "committed the Department of Education to making the elimination of sexism in education a priority." Following a directive from the governor's office, the education secretary sent memoranda to all university and college presidents and deans, listing specific antidiscriminatory policies which would be enforced, including: development of women's studies as an integral part of the curriculum, including feminist literature in libraries, and elimination of all segregated classes and activities.

The Wisconsin Governor's Commission on the Status of Women has introduced a bill into the legislature which would require the Board of Regents to take steps integrating the student body of all undergraduate and graduate schools in the state university system, in an effort to insure that the percentage of women students more nearly reflects the Wisconsin population.

Dartmouth College recently became the last of the Ivy League schools to admit women as regular students, and is planning to admit some 800 women over the next four years. The nation's reputedly first women's athletic scholarship has been established at the University of Chicago. The scholarship is for full tuition, regardless of need, and became available to freshman women beginning in the autumn quarter, 1973. There is no stipulation that the recipient of the scholarship participate in varsity sports at the university.

The Air Force Academy has announced its intention to admit female cadets by 1975. Yale has increased its female enrollment by over 100 additional women in order to "work toward a better balance between the sexes in Yale College." The university also announced that it would abandon rigid admissions quotas for men and women and seek to achieve an eventual 3 to 2 ratio by recruiting efforts.

The faculty senate of New York State University at Buffalo has recommended that 50 percent of all new university appointments go to women or minority group members. Stanford University has created a Faculty Affirmative Action Fund, initially financed at $75,000, to provide a special means to increase the proportion of women and minority faculty.

Sarah Lawrence College has received a $140,000 grant from the Rockefeller Foundation for expansion of the master's degree program in women's studies at the college. "Plans are to develop the program into a model for the teaching of women's studies in colleges across the country." An ad hoc committee at the University of Minnesota has been set up to explore ways to establish a women's studies major. Perhaps this is in response to a recent report in *Women's Studies Newsletter* that more than a thousand women's studies courses are now offered in the nation's colleges and universities.

The rush to deny women their identity apart from the group continues at a fevered pace.

Despite all the haste, many institutions have been unable to move quickly enough to satisfy critics. The University of Michigan has been charged with sex discrimination by the Committee to Bring about Equal Opportunity in Athletics for Men and Women. The formal complaint to HEW points out that the school spends $2.6 million a year on men's athletics, but has no allocation for women's intercollegiate sports. The University of Michigan athletic director countered with the charge that the school spends more money on its nursing school "and you don't see any men there." No doubt this will soon be investigated.

Among the schools which have failed to move quickly enough to suit the *Zeitgeist* have been some 150 institutions in 33 states which have never been sexually integrated. Some have been reserved entirely for men, some entirely for women. These schools have now received a formal warning from the U.S. Office of Education, threatening withdrawal of all federal aid unless they open enrollment to both sexes immediately. Apparently no differences will be tolerated in the homogenized schools of the future.

Reverse Discrimination

In the midst of this sexist hysteria, the same reverse discrimination exists in quotas for women as in quotas for minorities. On campus after campus, the push to achieve hiring quotas based on sex has introduced a marked distortion and injustice to the hiring process. As one dean described the situation, "If you're a woman and preferably black, you can get any kind of job you want." President Robben Fleming of the University of Michigan has already agreed to engage female professors for 139 of the next 148 vacancies on the faculty. What this does for the job prospects of others, including minorities, should be self-evident.

What may be less evident is the impact which this and similar rulings are likely to have on academic standards. When only 13 percent of the doctorates in America are awarded to women, and when feminists on the campus are already advocating that women faculty members should be on a one-to-one basis with men, where are the qualified female faculty to be recruited to fill the positions? In a time of tight money and scarce resources on the campus, perhaps the champions of women's liberation do not intend to expand faculties so much as they intend to replace men with women. If so, presumably this would mean the discharge of nearly one-half of the male professors now employed. As one professor recently remarked, "Perhaps those chauvinist exiles could occupy posts in secondary schooling vacated by schoolmarms who desire elevation to professorial dignity."

At present, there are few signs that such questions of elementary justice or basic academic standards will be allowed to stand before the egalitarian juggernaut.

The Case for Women

Although we hear a great deal about discrimination against women, and though such discrimination undoubtedly exists in many quarters, it is interesting that only 8 percent of those women polled by the authors of a recent study, *Sex Discrimination against the American Working Woman*, thought themselves to be victims of discrimination. Perhaps the other 92 percent have recognized that steady progress has been made in according an even break to those women who choose to work. Certainly the professional position and pay of women in the academic world had already been progressing for years, in both relative and absolute terms. Perhaps the 92 percent are aware of the large number of women who have been able to distinguish themselves in academic life without special enabling legislation on their behalf. Perhaps the 92 percent also resist the tendency to homogenize their skills, energies, and personalities into an egalitarian group project.

Finally, the 92 percent may simply be exercising their prerogative to be women.

One of the most charming discussions of women and their place in society was first published in 1918. I refer to H. L. Mencken's *In Defense of Women*. Mencken pointed out several basic truths about the woman and her role and capacities that even the most ardent women's liberationist fails to consider only at great peril. In an essay which deserves a wider hearing today, Mencken pointed out that a lack of feminine participation in much of the world of commerce, industry, and education is less a matter of inability, or even prejudice, than it is a feminine reaction against the dull mechanical tricks of the trade that the present organization of society compels on the part of those who work for a living. As Mencken phrased it, "And that rebellion testifies to their intelligence. If they enjoyed and took pride in those tricks, and showed it by diligence and skill, they would be on all fours with. . ." the men of society. Mencken insisted that women are consistently more intelligent than their male counterparts:

> Women decide the larger questions of life correctly and quickly, not because they are lucky guessers, not because they are divinely inspired, not because they practice a magic inherited from savagery, but simply and solely because they have sense. They see at a glance what most

men could not see with searchlights and telescopes; they are at grips with the essentials of a problem before men have finished debating its mere externals. They are the supreme realists of the race. Men, too, sometimes have brains. But that is a rare, rare man, I venture, who is as subtly intelligent, as constantly sound in judgment, as little put off by appearances, as the average women of forty-eight.

Of course, Mencken was the supreme iconoclast. He was also the supreme individualist, who might be criticized in this case for speaking of women, rather than taking his persons, male or female, one at a time. But he may have been right:

Women do not lend themselves to be regimented as men do—men find no problem in goose-stepping. The most civilized man is simply that man who has been most successful in gagging and harnessing his honest and natural instincts.

If women were indeed sufficiently perceptive to have avoided the regimentation of their male counterparts throughout history, one hopes they will be able to retain such common sense and individuality in the years immediately ahead, at a time when sexism seems to have replaced such older egalitarian causes as the war on poverty or the race question, as a dominant theme of the day.

What is Equality?

There is a contradiction between the goal of an equal society and the methods of attaining it by means of unequal treatment of individuals.

Paul Seabury

I N A SOCIETY which has long emphasized the concept of equal justice under the law, our recent tendency has been to carry that original doctrine far beyond equality of rights, until our present goal demands equality of condition. Of course, men are no more created equal than any other member of the animal kingdom—life is always unequal. Neither the Declaration of Independence nor the Constitution ever stated or implied an equality of condition. The guarantee of the 14th Amendment that no state shall deprive any citizen of "equal protection of the laws'' is only another way of expressing what we in the American experience have viewed as each man's inherent right to equality in freedom under law.

The American experience has been consistent on that definition of equality. Even two such political rivals and crusty personalities as Thomas Jefferson and John Adams were in essential agreement on the point. Harkening back to the time they spent in the summer of 1776, laboring together in Philadelphia to produce the final version of the Declaration of Independence, Adams wrote to Jefferson nearly thirty years later:

> Inequalities of mind and body are so established by God Almighty in His constitution of human nature that no art or policy can ever plane them down to a level. I have never read reasoning more absurd, sophistry more gross...than the subtle labors of Helvetius and Rousseau to demonstrate the natural equality of mankind.

It has been the American insistence upon an equality measured in freedom, independence and opportunity that has characterized our system. It is the accompanying inequality of individual talents, given full play by the legal guarantee of equal opportunity, which has led to progress in religion, intellectual affairs, the production of material wealth, and the pursuit of individual meaning in life. The social advances which we take for granted have their origin in allowing the individual the opportunity to give full play to his creative resources. It is precisely that aspect of American life which is now so heavily under attack. The assault upon the merit principle today is present not only in higher education, but throughout American society as a whole. The real danger of the social engineering now under way is that the drive toward mediocrity reflected in Affirmative Action programming has behind it not only the full weight of the United States government, but the unthinking support of most molders of public opinion. One reason for this may be that equality of opportunity, as opposed to equality of condition, lacks the political attractiveness necessary for success in an age of group-interest politics. However the situation came about, the fact remains that merit is today being scrapped in favor of quotas. In the process, mediocrity is being institutionalized and equal opportunity suppressed.

Education as the Panacea

In our society's fevered search for equality we have turned increasingly to education as the panacea for our politically induced guilt feelings and confusions on the subject of equality. The Affirmative Action mentality seems to suggest that if equality of condition does not exist, then it is the obligation of education so to mold future generations that such equality is finally produced. Naturally, education has failed to deliver the egalitarian dream, since the schools cannot hope to set aside the inequalities of individual condition. The egalitarians' response to this is to resort to compulsion, using legal force and political interventions to bring the schools to heel.

This tendency to politicize education in the name of a false equality has been under way for some time. The U.S. Office of Education reports that roughly two million of the fifty-one million school children in America are "gifted," but the same report goes on to suggest that very few of these talented youngsters are being properly educated in our public schools. Nearly a century and a half ago, Alexis de Tocqueville pointed out that something of the sort was likely to happen in America, since democracies tend to resent and resist inequalities of talent.

One of those avenues of society most open to achievers of real talent has been the academic community. Those gifted students who survived the drudgery common to many elementary and secondary schools have at least had the opportunity to distinguish themselves in the higher learning. It is this avenue of performance which Affirmative Action now moves to close in the name of a politically enforced egalitarian dream.

Keeping pace with this trend toward politicized education has been the frantic search for "scientific" sociological proof of our newfangled egalitarian assumptions. The sociological speculations of Brown *vs.* Board of Education seemed to promise some hope for the achievement of our politicized egalitarian goals, but the evidence which has accumulated since that time has been embarrassing to say the least. The 1966 Coleman Report on the "Equality of Educational Opportunity" was the first of several studies demonstrating that scholastic achievement of students is not a matter of the quality of the schools they attend.

The Coleman Report stunned the environmental determinists. Then Christopher Jencks produced *Inequality: A Reassessment of the Effect of Family and Schooling in America,* demonstrating once again that economic inequality did not have a significant effect on educational inequality in America. According to Jencks, inequality is recreated anew in each generation. Thus the search for equality of condition can be fulfilled only by stifling the creative capacities of those who would be most productive in each new generation. One would suspect that this would hardly be in the interest of the body politic as a whole, but we must remember that policies are made by politicians, and that politicians often create their issues in areas of mythology rather than fact.

The effort to attain egalitarian goals in education has continued to receive growing criticism on a number of fronts. Many of those in the vanguard of the egalitarian thrust of the 1960s have begun to have their doubts in the 1970s. Those egalitarians who continue to have the courage of their convictions, despite all evidence to the contrary—such men as John Rawls, author of the recently published *A Theory of Justice*—are at least willing to take the process to its logical conclusion. Mr. Rawls suggests that the egalitarian ideal cannot succeed in education until enforced redistribution of wealth and total regimentation of society first destroys all special advantages in position or talent. At least Mr. Rawls is honest enough to admit that equality of result is fundamentally incompatible with equality of opportunity.

Can we achieve equality through education? The battle now rages, with such participants as Jencks, Moynihan, Coleman, Pettigrew, and Jensen. Whatever other generalizations might be made about the egalitarian ideal and its connection with education, it seems clear that the intellectual assumptions on which the egalitarian ideal has been built in modern America are losing support among the very social scientists who provided much of the ideological thrust for the idea in the period between 1930 and 1970.

Assault on the Merit Principle

Although fewer social scientists advocate egalitarianism today, the political, popularized version of the idea is just now coming into its own. Federal administrative involvement in higher education has been paralleled by a growing involvement on the part of the courts. Since 1955, nearly 4,000 decisions affecting education have been handed down by this country's higher courts. In some of these decisions, especially those of recent vintage, the egalitarian intent is unmistakable. For example, a recent federal district court decision abolished the "track system" in the Washington, D.C. public schools. The track system is a device to allow all the children in a given school to operate on their own level of aptitude and performance. The program was ruled illegal and discriminatory since there were proportionately more white children in the higher tracks, and so the program had to go. Education in the public schools of Washington, D.C. has now been made safe for egalitarian mediocrity.

The courts are handing down similar decisions under new Affirmative Action rulings. Mark DeFunis, a white student making application to the University of Washington law school, was denied admission even though thirty-eight black students with significantly lower qualifications were admitted as members of the same class. DeFunis, an honors graduate of the University of Washington, brought suit on the grounds that his rights had been violated under the 14th Amendment. He was denied satisfaction by the state supreme court, in a decision which reeked of the egalitarian lust to remake society. Denying that DeFunis' higher entrance scores and grades were relevant, the court went on to say:

> It can hardly be gainsaid that the minorities have been, and are, grossly underrepresented in the law schools— and consequently in the legal profession—of this state and this nation. We believe the state has an overriding interest in promoting integration in public education. In light of the serious underrepresentation of minority

groups in the law schools, and considering that minority groups participate on an equal basis in the tax support of the law school, we find the state interest in eliminating racial imbalance within public legal education to be compelling.

It has been suggested that the minority admissions policy is not necessary, since the same objective could be accomplished by improving the elementary and secondary education of minority students to a point where they could secure equal representation in law schools, through direct competition with nonminority applicants on the basis of the same academic criteria. This would be highly desirable, but 18 years have passed since the decision Brown *vs.* Board of Education, and minority groups are still grossly underrepresented in law schools. If the law school is forbidden from taking affirmative action, this underrepresentation may be perpetuated indefinitely. No less restrictive means would serve the governmental interest here; we believe the minority admissions policy of the law school to be the only feasible "plan that promises realistically to work, and promises realistically to work *now.*"

"Work and...work now"—to remake the face of society. The court seems less interested in dispensing justice than in social engineering. In its decision we have a graphic sample of the Affirmative Action mentality in action.

Even if the egalitarian society were possible to achieve, the effort to attain it by unequal treatment of individuals is not likely to succeed; such methods would surely become the means which destroyed the end. We in America are just beginning to face the nature of this powerful dilemma. There are other nations in the world which, further down the road toward a presumed egalitarian goal, are discovering the same inescapable truth. When all the "reforms" desired in pursuit of the egalitarian dream become law as they have in Britain and Swe-

den, we have an opportunity to view the outcome
firsthand. The reforms have satisfied no one and settled
nothing. In Irving Kristol's words, "Above all, the pas-
sion for equality, so far from having been appeased, has
been exacerbated, so that there is more bitter controversy
over equality—and more inequalities—in Sweden and
Britain today than was the case 5 or 10 years ago."

The Indian experience also gives firsthand evidence
of the final destination of the egalitarian dream. Nehru at-
tempted to establish equality in the new-style egalitarian
manner, institutionalizing reverse discrimination as the
means to his end. What happened was that the disadvantaged beneficiaries of quotas came to view their situation
as a prescriptive right, while more and more Indians
sought "the previous designation of backwardness" as a
means of gaining privilege. Once established, quotas tend
to perpetuate themselves.

What women, blacks, social engineers and all the
rest of us might keep in mind as we examine the slogans
of the day, especially those slogans of an egalitarian variety, is Aristotle's old point that a just and legitimate society is one in which inequalities—of property, or station
or power—are generally perceived by the citizenry as
necessary for the common good. At best, it is always difficult for a society to retain a sufficient sense of balance
to work toward the common good and not be turned aside
into empty political promises concerning absolute equality
of condition. The corrective balance which kept this nation and much of Western civilization on the right track
has always been what Irving Kristol describes as the
"common sense" of the majority of the population. It is
that common sense which is under such heavy attack today.

One reason we suffer an erosion of common sense
may lie in the fact that we are generating a larger and

larger class of "intellectuals." The intellectual, as the word is increasingly used today, is not merely the man who uses his intellect—we all do that, to greater or lesser degree. An intellectual is best defined as a person whose work demands that he devote the bulk of his time and attention to abstract issues apart from the normal business of daily life that occupies most men. For this reason, or for some reason, today's intellectual class is deeply alienated from American society, feeling itself superior to the common man, and above the whole process of getting and spending. Thus many intellectuals are sharply critical of the world they see around them, generally regarding that world as unfair and unjust because they feel it does not provide them with an equal status in society. In fact, the status of the intellectual is high indeed in our present society. He is able to live well and pursue his own interests in a fashion never before possible. Despite this, the theme of "inequality" persists. Those providing most of the leadership toward enforced equality, toward what is now called Affirmative Action, prove to be members of the academic community and the professions. Yet a special irony lies in the fact that these reformers have now set in motion a process which subjects the standards and practices of their institutions to heavy attack from the newly empowered egalitarian bureaucracy they helped to create.

The Fist of Government

Stanley Lowell, former chairman of the New York City Commission on Human Rights, made a statement some time ago which indicates how far the doctrinaire can go in pursuit of the egalitarian goal: "The time has come when color consciousness is necessary and appropriate....The protection of human rights needs the fist of government." When we look to government for protection of human rights, we are relying upon an agency which has a very bad track record in defending anyone's rights. I suspect that very often when we invoke the power of government, we are acting in the belief that we have discovered some cause so noble it justifies using organized force to insure compliance on the part of our less enlightened fellow citizens, who otherwise might not cooperate. But there is scarcely any means of reform less effective than compulsion. The Affirmative Action zealots are already learning to their sorrow that the bureaucratic solution is worse than no solution at all.

Meanwhile, there is serious confusion at the heart of the egalitarian ideal. The thrust of Affirmative Action in all its forms is toward the homogenized society in which all are absolutely equal, and yet the means of attainment is to be through special group identity. We are all to be made identical by treating various interest groups in nonidentical ways, giving some privilege and discriminating against others.

At the same time, the priorities among interest groups are continually shifting. The lust for Affirmative Action has caused a sharp decline in the intensity of feeling toward earlier causes. Not too long ago, the "poor" were presumably the central problem of our times. Now we hear very little about the subject. Race is also giving way to sex as the "trendy" cause.

Pursuit of Opportunity

Somewhere out there among all the fashionable causes, the old ideal of individual opportunity and identity has been lost. Politicized egalitarian rhetoric and enforced quotas cannot restore that opportunity. So long as we treat ironclad, legally enforced group membership as the key to solving our problems, we may rest assured that individual opportunity will be progressively harder to rediscover.

Perhaps the problem in America is our success. In this nation the common man has generally enjoyed a substantial opportunity to do something for himself and his family. He has gone to work and built an astonishing level of prosperity, both in the wealth created and in the numbers of people sharing in that wealth. Surely this was the fruit of genuine individual opportunity. The system worked, but perhaps in working it created new appetites. Perhaps we were caught in an escalating world of achievement and expectation—the more we had, the more we wanted. Tocqueville told us to expect as much:

> Among democratic nations men easily attain a certain equality of conditions: they can never attain the equality they desire. It perpetually retires before them, yet without hiding itself from their sight, and in retiring draws them on. . . .
>
> When inequality of conditions is the common law of society, the most marked inequalities do not strike the eye: when everything is nearly on the same level, the slightest are marked enough to hurt it. Hence the desire of equality always becomes more insatiable in proportion as equality is more complete.

Despite our problems, one of the central facts of American history has been the achievement of a high de-

gree of individual equality for most citizens. Perhaps the
nation somehow sensed that human beings achieve their
fulfillment in what they become. Certainly we are most
fully ourselves as we aspire to further development, and
enjoy the freedom to pursue it. It is in connection with
our aspiration that we seek equality for each person.
Surely race or sex is an inadequate basis for such equality. We do not aspire to be black, white, or yellow, male
or female. These categories are facts of existence, but the
achievement which we seek in life must lie elsewhere,
and it is elsewhere that the definition of true equality
must also be located.

What we all want, and what some members of society presently lack, is acceptance as an individual by others. It is that acceptance which constitutes genuine
equality. Each of us wants to be a person in his own
right. Such acceptance can hardly be produced by governmental compulsion. Compulsion smothers any creative response to a problem.

Quotas undercut acceptance for the individual. No
matter how many legal guarantees enforce the quota, the
primary effect is a stoppage of the acceptance and the opportunities for individual development which we seek. If
a person lacks qualification for a position, it is a disser-
vice to that person and to society as a whole to enforce a
quota and compel legal acceptance. Quotas limit rather
than enhance opportunity; they degrade rather than digni-
fy. And as one pastor of a Harlem church put it, speaking
for all quota-entrapped groups, "If we are going to be
judged without discrimination then we will also be judged
without pity." The only equality with real meaning is
that based upon an absence of prejudgment. The quota is
itself a prejudgment, institutionalized with the force of
law, standing as a permanent obstacle to true equality.

Perhaps the route toward alleviation of our present discontents lies through a restatement and redefinition of the equality we seek. A vast majority of us want genuine equality of opportunity for all citizens. Discrimination on the grounds of race, sex, religion, or any other group-oriented basis is simply unacceptable. But the course we now pursue is calculated to enforce a peculiarly American version of apartheid, an apartheid which not only sets race apart, but adds sex as another category of public regulation.

By every standard of simple equity, by the standards of the American dream at its best, in the interest of all individuals, especially in the interest of the "disadvantaged," and finally in the interest of society as a whole, we must understand that the egalitarian dream now pursued by Affirmative Action programming on the campuses of America's colleges and universities is undercutting the very structure of the open society. The commendable quest for equality of opportunity must not be confused with the shoddy, politicized quotas of Affirmative Action.

Education vs. Egalitarian Politics

...there cannot be a university or college anywhere in the country today that does not know that where basic grievances exist, those who are aggrieved will turn to every available source for redress, including the federal government. And surely they must know that if the university does not *voluntarily* deal with the issue, a vacuum is created which the government, like nature, abhors.

J. Stanley Pottinger

N O ONE FAMILIAR with the bureaucratic mentality can be surprised to learn that Stanley Pottinger regards the power of the Office of Civil Rights to be on a par with the forces of nature. For that matter, Pottinger may be right. Already the Affirmative Action bureaucracy has so proliferated that the HEW "Contract Compliance" force alone has nearly 500 employees. And yet HEW is still not moving fast enough for some of the zealots. A coalition of various minority groups has charged that current guidelines "undercut and dilute" civil rights enforcement.

Such groups need not be concerned. It seems a fore-
gone conclusion that more comprehensive and stringent
pressures are on the way. The federal bureaucracy is sup-
plemented by various state level actions. These state bu-
reaucracies have moved to enforce changes in faculty
hiring and promotion, curricular offerings, housing,
hours, and other aspects of campus business in both public and private higher educational institutions. Worst of
all, there is a sort of "do-it-yourself" Affirmative Action
in operation on many campuses, where the administrators
are running ahead of specific HEW guidelines in an anxious effort to avoid trouble.

All this is in addition to the main thrust of federal
Affirmative Action, which continues to accelerate. The
President's budget request for fiscal 1974 contained a
substantial increase for the Office of Civil Rights. Some
sixty new positions have been created in the office, pro-
ducing a newly formed Division of Higher Education
with the special responsibility of enforcing the executive
order against sex bias in colleges and universities. Meanwhile, the Equal Employment Opportunity Commission,
which already has jurisdiction over all educational institutions (whether or not they receive federal funds) is pro-
jecting a budgetary increase of nearly 50 percent, to a
total of some $43,000,000. The United States Commis-
sion of Civil Rights, which now has enlarged jurisdiction
including sex discrimination and is currently planning an
investigation of bias on the campus, will receive an increase of some 13 percent in its budget.

Both the Equal Employment Opportunity Commission and the Equal Pay Division of the Department of Labor have also been cooperating with HEW campus
investigations. A number of cases involving salary discrimination have already been pressed, both in and out of

court. Suits have been filed against the University of Pittsburgh, the University of California at Berkeley, the University of Maryland, and Florida State University. The Florida State suit involves nine women faculty members suing the institution for $1 million in back pay and damages. These pressures have caused deans to take out personal liability insurance, since individual administrators may be expected to be named in an increasing number of suits.

Small wonder that the academic community is running scared. This climate of fear, generated by reverse discrimination against individuals and increasing governmental interference in the affairs of our colleges and universities, characterizes the present state of Affirmative Action on the American campus.

Of perhaps still greater consequence for the future is the development of a new federal agency, the National Institute of Education, with the announced function to promote basic research in the processes of learning and teaching. As one university president has remarked:

> When a federal institution begins finding the best methods of teaching, and is also associated with unrestricted support for instructional programs in colleges and universities, it is just a matter of time—and a short time at that—until the conclusions of the institute on how teaching *ought* to be done are going to come over as requirements for those institutions that are receiving aid. These additional *requirements* will inevitably reach into the most sensitive area of the educational process—the content and manner of teaching.

The United States Office of Education has recently announced that it is engaged in developing new standards to apply to those organizations which accredit colleges and universities. Accreditation is a major factor in higher education. Without it, a school cannot hire qualified faculty, cannot guarantee students that scholastic work will be recognized on a transfer basis by other institutions, and indeed probably cannot long survive in the present academic climate.

And now it is proposed by the U.S. Office of Education that this life and death power of accreditation be made subject to a single national pattern. One of the suggested items in this new pattern would be that accrediting agencies have "ethical standards for institutions and programs in such areas as discrimination in admissions and hiring...."

Such total federal control for all schools, whether or not they receive federal funds, is not far down the road. The National Institute of Education has already received an initial grant of $92 million to facilitate research and central planning for the new national programs.

Disregard for Basic Legal Guarantees

Another highly disturbing aspect of the present rush toward Affirmative Action has been the cavalier attitude adopted toward traditional legal guarantees. The OCR tendency has been to dismiss those abuses of legal rights which have arisen in A.A. programs on many campuses as mere "excesses of zeal" on the part of local officials. In June 1972, Stanley Pottinger publicly declared, "I am convinced...that the specter of lost autonomy and diminished quality among faculties is one which obscures the real objective of the law against discrimination." As one commentator has observed, Pottinger seems to be implying that a law's consequences should not be allowed to "obscure" the intentions of its maker. For the zealot, good intentions are always enough. Presumably we may then overlook the harmful consequences of such laws.

And harmful consequences there are in abundance with Affirmative Action. For example, one of the root assumptions of Anglo-American jurisprudence has been that the accused is innocent until proven guilty. Not so with Affirmative Action, which assumes the educational institution guilty of discrimination until the school proves its innocence. Personnel records, previously considered confidential, are now regarded as fair game in Affirmative Action investigations, with no interest whatsoever displayed by the bureaucracy in securing permission from the persons whose personal files are thus converted into public property.

Affirmative Action pressures are also generating some highly questionable legal tendencies among the college and university administrators. Not long ago a document was circulated at a meeting of the Northeast Regional Group on Student Affairs of the Association of American Medical Colleges, by the associate dean of a leading university in New York, recommending to fellow administrators a means for avoidance of moral and legal problems which might arise in reverse discrimination cases involving student admissions and faculty hiring. The dean described his secret consultation with several members of the judiciary, in which means were discussed whereby provisions for admission and hiring could "get around" constitutional and legal obstacles to reverse discrimination:

> The purpose. . . is to explore in as concise a fashion as possible prevailing legal attitudes and how several distin-

guished jurists view this irksome problem. The heart of
the matter is how the courts will treat the problem if and
when presented with it, and their response, which may not
be consistent, is the only tangible and dependable support
available. Five justices of the New York State Supreme
Court were identified for consultation. Three judges spent
a considerable amount of their time discussing their own
and what they thought the court's ultimate response
would be to a law suit similar to the one now before the
Supreme Court of the State of Washington....

Such collusion is clearly illegal as well as morally
unacceptable. These same judges may one day hear such
cases, and yet they are the same men now giving advice
or the best means to deny redress for reverse discriminatory practices.

As a part of the same document described above, the
associate dean admitted the intent of his recommendation
was a quota system under another name:

Establishing given percentages or quotas of minority students to be accepted in a class represents predictable
problems. This should be avoided at all costs. It is possible to achieve the same results without giving the appearance of restricting portions of the class for designated
groups.

When representatives of higher education and members of the legal profession, including judges seated in responsible positions, meet in deliberate attempts to bypass
legal guarantees for individuals penalized by the new reverse discrimination, the whole process becomes even
more reprehensible.

Administrators today are also faced with the necessi-
ty of *deciding which law they will disobey:* the 1964 Civil Rights Act forbidding discrimination, or the
Affirmative Action guidelines which carry the force of
law and which specifically require discrimination on the

basis of race and sex. In such a climate, it is not difficult to understand the confusion and lack of principle which characterize so many Affirmative Action programs.

The Latest Application of an Old Idea

The quota system is far from a new idea. It is not the wave of the future; it is the putrid backwash of all the tired social engineering schemes of centuries. Both the Communists and the Nazis made prominent use of quotas recently enough that we should have no trouble remembering the result.

A departmental chairman in a large Eastern state university circulated a letter to a number of other departmental chairmen across the country, asking that the *curricula vitae* of new Ph.D.'s contain identifications of race and sex, since HEW hiring orders were impossible to follow in the absence of such information. To his credit, one of the departmental chairmen of a Western university replied:

> If there were objective or legally established definitions of race, together with a legal requirement of full disclosure of racial origins, we would be in the clear. I understand that a number of steps in this direction were achieved by the ''Nuremberg laws'' of Nazi Germany. And in the Soviet Union, I am told, all individuals carry their racial identifications on their internal passports. Similarly for blacks in South Africa. So there are precedents.
>
> I would suggest that the American Economic Association call upon the Department of Health, Education, and Wel-

fare (HEW) and other bureaucratic agencies now engaged in promoting racial discrimination for assistance. We should ask them to establish legal "guidelines" as to: (1) which races are to be preferred, and which discriminated against; (2) what criteria (how many grandparents?) determine racial qualifications for employment; (3) what administrative procedures must be set up for appeals against arbitrary classification.

With guidelines like these, you and other department chairmen would suffer neither embarrassment nor inconvenience in employing some individuals, and refusing to hire others, on the grounds of their race and sex. And you will have the peace of mind of knowing that the authenticity of racial labelings have in effect been guaranteed by an agency of the federal government.

If the President of the United States has the power to command colleges and universities to establish faculty quotas on the basis of race and sex, why not faculty quotas on the basis of ideology or party membership? Unless we answer definitely the questions concerning which portions of society are public and which are private, our inevitable tendency will be toward the totally politicized state.

Today federal power within the academy has already grown to life and death proportions. Federal funding already provides great leverage. The situation seems well on the way, through a variety of channels, to applying the same pressures to all colleges and universities, whether or not they receive federal money. This seems to be the assumption of much federal policy. Elliot Richardson, former secretary of HEW, defended Affirmative Action by claiming it was the federal government's vital interest to assure "the largest possible pool of qualified manpower for its project." As Professor Paul Seabury immediately asked, "Does HEW now regard universities as federal projects? If so, how far down the road of govern-

ment control have we come?'' In view of all the pressures discussed in these pages, pressures involving
funding, accreditation, admissions, faculty hiring, and
nearly every other aspect of campus life, to be adminis-
tered by a variety of federal agencies, parallel state agencies, and the courts, it seems clear that we have come a
long way indeed.

Not only is the power of self-determination passing
from the academy, but in many cases the rise of Affirmative Action is destroying quality and standards as well.
Higher education must have no priority ahead of the
search for truth and the perfection of learning standards.
When ''social justice'' supplants these goals within the
academy, the result is likely to be a misdirection of attention and scarce resources from the primary goal of education. One effect of that misdirection has been the
extremely expensive administrative costs which accompa-
ny Affirmative Action. One small college president announced: ''To tell you the truth, my little college simply
does not have the personnel to go through all our records
and do the necessary homework.'' The Office of Civil
Rights investigator replied: ''Too bad. You'll just have to
dig up somebody to do it.''

The briefest examination of a completed Affirmative
Action plan should make it abundantly clear how high the
costs are in preparation of the original material. It has
been estimated by the business manager of a large Mid-
western university that $1 million would be necessary to
make the transition to the new set of records and procedures demanded by Affirmative Action on his campus.
This figure does not include the continuing costs involved
in the maintenance and monitoring of an Affirmative Action program.

One academic investigator deeply involved in study-
ing the impact of Affirmative Action programs on a num-

ber of campuses conservatively estimates that an ongoing Affirmative Action program, operated within HEW guidelines, would consume 50 percent of the total administrative budget of a typical school. At a time when resources for higher education promise to be in increasingly short supply in the years ahead, such administrative costs are likely to have a great impact, probably further increasing dependence upon political funding.

Another problem arising within the academy as the direct result of Affirmative Action is the application of improper measurement standards, standards unsuitable to higher education. The language and practices developed by the Labor Department for application of Affirmative Action programs in industry have been imitated by HEW and applied to higher education. There should be recognizable difference between a plumbers' union and a faculty. There is also the vital difference that the university is a highly decentralized institution which HEW now proposes to administer not only as though each school were a tightly knit unit, but also as though all schools were nothing more than interchangeable units of "the education industry." Such standards cannot be applied without doing lasting harm.

Lowered standards in admissions and faculty hiring, induced by HEW standards and such bizarre notions as the "qualifiable" candidate, will also inevitably have an effect throughout all segments of higher education. It should be obvious that the hiring of a faculty member, on any other basis than the particular merit of that individual faculty member, must in the long run be prejudicial to the quality of the institutional faculty so affected. The responsibility of every faculty and administration in this country is to find the most qualified person available for a particular post, regardless of race, sex, religion, or national origin. Any other basis for selection is not only discriminatory, but must necessarily be a downward step in the quality of the institution.

The same situations apply for admissions policies in academic institutions. Those institutions which have experimented with lowering their admissions standards to achieve racial balance have then found that the students admitted under the lower standards can only be retained in school if the institution is willing to lower its classroom standards as well. As in the case of discriminatory hiring, discriminatory admissions practices work directly contrary to the ideal of quality education.

Perhaps one of the most saddening aspects of the entire affair is the special damage which Affirmative Action inflicts upon the very people for whose benefit the program presumably operates. The hiring of professors or the admission of students on any other basis than ability works a particular hardship on the "favored" groups. The qualified, achieving students and teachers can never be sure of where they stand. How can one build an academic standing when neither he nor his colleagues will ever know for sure whether he is there because of ability or because he was part of some racial or sexual quota? The unqualified student or professor fares even worse. Such a person can be retained only by lowering standards and thus cheating those involved of the education they have been promised.

Proper Function of a University

The vagaries of politically pursued egalitarian dreams are hard to follow. We have considered the effects of Affirmative Action on individuals, black and white, man and woman. We have considered the effects of Affirmative Action on the various groups within society. Perhaps an appropriate closing note might be a brief look at the impact of Affirmative Action on society as a whole. Here are the thoughts of Professor Paul Seabury of the University of California at Berkeley, one of the outspoken and highly effective critics of Affirmative Action:

> The case for merit and equal opportunity must also be seen in the light of common standards of a complex society which, after all, depends on the skills of the individuals composing it. Concerns of human safety, convenience, and the quality of our collective life are of as great consequence as our concern for equal protection of the laws. We do want a qualified surgeon when we need an operation. We assume we want a skilled pilot, especially when it is we who are on the plane. We want a clever lawyer when we are in trouble. We want the telephone to work, and our mail to come to us, and not to someone down the street. We want competent teachers for our children. In universities we want high standards of scholarship and research and we want them visible also as exemplars of excellence. In short, we want the entire complex of amenities and necessities in a condition which we can reasonably trust. Our existence places us at the mercy of persons, often invisible to us, who are certified for their qualities. While we may quibble about the arbitrary and fallible manner in which, in real life, skill and competence may be ascertained, we would hardly therefore argue that such standards are worthless, or that better ones could not be devised. Yet the erosion of standards, in the name of a form of equity, risks lowering the quality of existence and experience.

The merit system, which has made possible the retention of those norms permitting society to function effectively, has enjoyed an especially important place within the academic community. At its best, the academic community has consistently reflected a standard of professional excellence which is truly egalitarian. The egalitarianism of excellence offered opportunity for those able and willing to compete, with countless spin-off benefits to society deriving from that excellence. Now what is at stake in Affirmative Action programming is the end of that true equality of opportunity and the end of that excellence.

If we give way before the force which now menaces higher education and our society as a whole, we are not only opening the door to second-rate standards and a new and more vicious and permanent form of injustice. We are also passing control of tomorrow's leaders and tomorrow's dominant ideas from the privacy and independence of the academic community to the realm of egalitarian politics. If Affirmative Action gains the final say in curriculum, faculty, and admissions throughout higher education, effective control of society will have passed to the social engineers and the politicians, and America will have lost one of her greatest resources in the struggle to remain an open and effective society.

George C. Roche III

Before becoming the eleventh president of Hillsdale College in Hillsdale, Michigan, in 1971, George Charles Roche III was for five years director of seminars at the Foundation for Economic Education in Irvington-on-Hudson, New York. Before that, he taught history and philosophy at the Colorado School of Mines in Golden, Colorado.

A native of Colorado, President Roche grew up in the Rockies and until the eighth grade, he attended a one-room schoolhouse. After receiving his A.B. in history from Denver's Regis College, he spent two years as a Marine Corps officer. His M.A. and Ph.D.—both in history—are from the University of Colorado, where he also taught for a year.

As a senior member of the FEE staff, Dr. Roche spoke often before foundation seminars, industrial seminars, and professional groups, as well as on college and university campuses all across America. In a normal year he traveled a hundred thousand miles defending private property, free enterprise, and individual freedom.

Dr. Roche is a member of the American Historical Association, the Philadelphia Society, the Textbook Evaluation Committee of *America's Future,* the Mont Pelerin Society, the National Advisory Board of Young Americans for Freedom, and the American Academy of Political and Social Science. He is also a consultant to the Center for Independent Education, vice president of the American Association of Presidents of Independent Colleges and Universities, chairman of the Academic Advisory Council of the Charles Edison Memorial Youth Fund, a member of the Advisory Council of the Freedom Education Committee of the American Association of Physicians and Surgeons, and a member of the board of directors of the Qualpeco Corporation of New York City. In 1972, Dr. Roche received the Freedom Leadership Award of Freedoms Foundation, Valley Forge, Pennsylvania.

President Roche is a contributing editor of two magazines, *Private Practice* and *The St. Croix Review.* He writes a nationally distributed newspaper column, and his magazine articles have appeared in numerous publications.

Dr. Roche is also the author of four books: *Education in America, Legacy of Freedom, Frederic Bastiat: A Man Alone,* and *The Bewildered Society.*

Dr. and Mrs. Roche are the parents of a son, George Charles Roche IV, 18; and two daughters, Muriel Eileen, 3; and Margaret Clare born in May 1973. The Roche family lives in Broadlawn, traditional home of Hillsdale College presidents.

TRADITION AND REFORM IN EDUCATION

STEPHEN TONSOR

Michigan's Professor Tonsor has cast his historian's eye on the chaotic colleges of the sixties. What is needed, he believes, is drastic reform. Here he proposes radical changes in the way higher education is funded; argues for the restoration of those values of the spirit that promote true intellectual growth. And he devotes a section to the dilemmas of Catholic colleges and concludes that they have a particularly vital role because they have never surrendered the basic values by which men need to live.

ISBN 0-87548-124-8
Cloth   250 pages   6 x 9
$8.95

- - - - - - - - - - - - - - - - - - - -

ORDER FORM

Open Court
Box 599
La Salle, Ill. 61301

Please send me postpaid _____ copies of _____

_____. I enclose _____.

Name _____

Address _____

City _____ State _____ Zip Code _____

THE 12-YEAR SENTENCE
WILLIAM F.
RICKENBACKER (ed.)

"Examines the controversy over compulsory education from historical, biological, legal (both federal and state), sociological, political, and economic viewpoints. . . . One of the best presently available."
—*Library Journal*

"These writers agree broadly that forcing a child to attend school—in the context of the "cookie-cutter" kind of operation which prevails today—amounts to a 'sentence' for the child rather than an opportunity to learn. The failures of so many public schools are brought home graphically to the reader."
—*Publishers Weekly*

ISBN 0-87548-152-3
236 pages Cloth
Legal and General bibliographies
$6.95

ORDER FORM

Open Court
Box 599
La Salle, Ill. 61301

Please send me postpaid _____ copies of _____

_____. I enclose _____.

Name _____

Address _____

City _____ State _____ Zip Code _____

THE FALL OF THE AMERICAN UNIVERSITY

ADAM ULAM

"... a scintillating critique, in the names of commonsense, learning and joy, of the muddle-headed which, Professor Ulam seriously fears, is destroying what is really valuable in American universities."
—*Times Literary Supplement*

ISBN 0-912050-20-90
220 pages Cloth
$7.95

- - - - - - - - - - - - - - -

ORDER FORM

Open Court
Box 599
La Salle, Ill. 61301

Please send me postpaid _____ copies of _____

_____. I enclose _____.

Name _____

Address _____

City _____ State _____ Zip Code _____

THE USES OF A LIBERAL EDUCATION

BRAND BLANSHARD

"Blanshard has taught philosophy at Yale, Swarthmore and elsewhere, but is revealed in this book as a generalist in the humanities who takes all knowledge as his field. . . . He also ranges widely through other subjects, such as British scholarship, art, and—thanks be—the pleasures to be found in books. Recommended."—*John Barkham Reviews*

"It is particularly refreshing and timely that a defense of the liberal education should appear; it is equally refreshing that some of the fads of 'relevancy' and 'innovation' should be put in their place."—*Library Journal*

**ISBN 0-87548-122-1
415 pages   Index   Cloth
$9.95**

- - - - - - - - - - - - - - - - - - -

ORDER FORM

Open Court
Box 599
La Salle, Ill. 61301

Please send me postpaid _____ copies of _____

_____. I enclose _____.

Name _____

Address _____

City _____ State _____ Zip Code _____

THE BALANCING ACT
QUOTA HIRING IN HIGHER EDUCATION

Dr. George C. Roche III

"What ultimately is at stake in this issue of Affirmative Action is the institutional integrity of higher education. If America's institutions of higher learning lose control over who attends the schools and who teaches in them—their standards of excellence will inevitably be compromised."

Affirmative Action now threatens to take control of hiring and admissions procedures from colleges and universities in the country, replacing it with "guidelines" which amount to a quota system. Dr. George Roche, president of Hillsdale College in Michigan, raises a clear and determined voice in defense of individuals, judged solely on the basis of their individual merit.

The Office of Civil Rights and the Department of Health, Education and Welfare are now pressuring institutions of higher learning into compliance with the thinly veiled threat of withheld government funding. Failure to comply with the "guidelines" and "goals" jeopardizes 2,500 of 3,000 campuses across the country which depend on government dollars.

Order form

Additional copies of THE BALANCING ACT: Quota Hiring in Higher Education may be ordered from Hillsdale College, Hillsdale, Michigan 49242.

Single copy	$1.00	Name _____
Five copies	.85 each	Address _____
Ten copies	.75 each	_____ Zip _____
25 copies	.65 each	No. of copies _____ Price _____
More than 25	.60 each	Michigan residents add 4% tax ____
(All sent to same address)		Total enclosed _____

Please make checks payable to Hillsdale College.